McKinsey Quarterly

Government and business: New rules for

2009
Number 3

The new normal

Ian Davis

The case for government reform now

François Bouvard,
Thomas Dohrmann, and
Nick Lovegrove

Reforming the public sector in a crisis:

An interview with Sweden's former prime minister

Alastair Levy
and Nick Lovegrove

26
The current economic downturn has shown itself to be fundamentally different from recessions of the recent past. What we are experiencing is not merely another turn in the business cycle, but a restructuring of the economic order.

While no one can say how long the crisis will last, what we find on the other side will not look like the normal of recent years but a "new normal" in which the government will play an expanded role. Significant regulatory restructuring and demanding new levels of transparency will greatly impact sectors that were once subject to a lighter touch. Executives preparing their organizations to succeed in this new environment must focus on what has changed and what essentially remains the same for their customers, companies, and industries.

29
Governments are now intervening to an unprecedented degree in private markets and assuming tasks beyond the scope of traditional policy and public services.

More than ever, the public sector must discharge its functions efficiently and effectively. But few governments have an established track record or a reputation for managerial excellence. When they try reforms, they typically skim the surface, cover too little ground, take too long, and leave much of their structure relatively untouched.

The public sector must pursue a whole-government transformation by broadening, deepening, and accelerating reform. The current crisis provides both the need and the opportunity to improve the machinery of the state in a fundamental way.

39
Former Swedish prime minister Göran Persson describes in an interview how his government put state finances in order and reformed the huge public sector as his country suffered from a deep crisis similar to the one unfolding in the world today.

Persson, who came to power in 1996, when unemployment had risen threefold and the budget deficit tenfold, reflects on what it takes to win sustained public and political support for a harsh but ultimately successful crisis program and on how to drive efficiencies and service improvements across government.

Government and business: New rules for a new era

New challenges for Asia's governments

David Skilling

Special report: Inside the US stimulus program

Weighing the US government's response to the crisis: A dialogue

Allen P. Webb

47
Across the world, the role of government is expanding and changing. That's likely to happen in Asia, too, as new challenges and opportunities emerge.

Specifically, governments are likely to assume a more prominent role as principal investors, alliance builders, and economic strategists. These changes create an urgent need for Asian governments to transform their capacity and performance.

50
Introduction:
Implications for three industries

Joshua Crossman, Fred Kneip, and Jon Wilkins

53
Energy:
Investing in efficiency

Scott Jacobs and Rob McNish

56
Health care:
Taking medical records online

Sanjeev Agarwal, Brian Milch, and Steve Van Kuiken

59
Broadband:
Improving access

Joshua Crossman, Dilip Wagle, and Jon Wilkins

61
The extraordinary government response to the financial crisis has enormous implications for companies. In this conversation, two strategic thinkers—Lowell Bryan, a director in McKinsey's New York office, and Richard Rumelt, a professor of strategy at UCLA's Anderson School of Management—reflect on government's reactions to the crisis through the spring of 2009, and the resulting opportunities and threats they see on the horizon.

Feature article

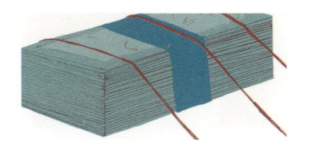

Energy, Resources, Materials

Learning from financial regulation's mistakes

Patrick Butler

Rebuilding corporate reputations

Sheila Bonini, David Court, and Alberto Marchi

Electrifying cars: How three industries will evolve

Russell Hensley, Stefan Knupfer, and Dickon Pinner

68
There's no shortage of proposals to prevent another crisis by improving the regulation of the global financial-services sector. Yet most of these ideas build on the existing regulatory system, which failed to anticipate or prevent the current problem and has done little to mitigate its impact.

Policy makers must consider fundamental change if they are to take advantage of this once-in-a-generation opportunity to overhaul the regulatory system. Otherwise, they could sow the seeds of the next calamity.

75
The financial crisis has reduced public trust in business and markets broadly—which is particularly problematic at a time when the relationship between business and government is changing fundamentally.

Companies must rebuild the social contract, reinvigorate relationships with their critical stakeholders, and redouble their efforts to stay on top of sector-specific issues—such as climate change, obesity, and worker safety—that could threaten their reputations.

To do so, companies should improve their understanding of reputational issues and stakeholders, emphasize transparency and action rather than spin, and move beyond PR in seeking to influence key constituents.

86
Electrified vehicles seem to be in the ascendant: nearly every major automaker has announced plans to launch some variety of electrified car. China, the United States, and other nations are committing huge sums to their development, and private investment is following.

How aggressively governments underwrite electrified vehicles will determine how long it takes for them to enter the mainstream. But when they do—in a few years or a couple of decades—these cars will spark structural changes in the auto and utilities sectors and give rise to a new battery industry. Executives should understand now what it will take to win in a battery-powered age.

Feature article

Marketing

The consumer decision journey

David Court, Dave Elzinga, Susan Mulder,
and Ole Jørgen Vetvik

96

Marketing has always sought to reach consumers at the moments that influence their decisions. For years, those opportunities were viewed through the metaphor of a purchasing "funnel," where consumers start with a number of brands in mind and emerge with their choice. Today, marketers require a more sophisticated approach to navigate a complex environment of proliferating products, fragmenting media, and increasingly discerning, well-informed consumers. We call this approach the *consumer decision journey*.

To adjust to the way consumers now make decisions, marketers will have to reinvigorate the customer experience, find new ways to ensure that their brands are considered, and develop innovative strategies for managing word-of-mouth. By understanding the consumer journey, marketers can ensure they are in the right place at the right time, providing the information and support consumers need to make their decisions.

Special section

Strategy/Corporate Finance

The crisis: Planning for uncertainty

109
M&A in a downturn: Timing strategic moves

Richard Dobbs
and Timothy M. Koller

Timing is key as companies weigh whether to make strategic investments now or wait for clear signs of recovery. Scenario analysis can expose the risks of moving too quickly or slowly.

115
Just-in-time budgeting for a volatile economy

Mahmut Akten, Massimo Giordano, and Mari A. Scheiffele

A volatile economy makes traditional budgets obsolete before they're even completed. Here's how companies can adapt more quickly.

122
Strategic planning in a crisis

Andrew Cheung, Eric Kutcher, and Dilip Wagle

Commentary from McKinsey experts and *Quarterly* readers

By Invitation

Economic Studies

How 'animal spirits' destabilize economies

George A. Akerlof and
Robert J. Shiller

126

Adam Smith saw that human beings rationally pursue their economic interests, and his economic theories explain what happens when they do. But they are also guided by noneconomic motives—animal spirits—which Smith and his followers largely ignore. That's why they hold that capitalism is essentially stable and has little need for government interference.

George Akerlof and Robert Shiller, on the contrary, believe that animal spirits play a significant and largely destabilizing role in the economy. Without government intervention, employment levels at times swing massively and financial markets fall into chaos.

Interview

Nonprofit

Developing entrepreneurs among the world's poorest:
An interview with Acumen Fund's founder

Bill Javetski

136
A finance leader turned social-sector pioneer, Jacqueline Novogratz has used her experience in finance to forge a new approach to philanthropy. Founded in 2001, Acumen Fund pairs public work with private investment to develop entrepreneurs in some of the world's poorest countries. In this interview, Novogratz discusses the opportunities and challenges that come with breaking the mold, and the unique perspective her experiences have given her on cross-sector innovation.

143
Reader comments on this article from mckinseyquarterly.com

Departments

This Quarter

7
The new business of government

On Our Web Site

8
Now available on mckinseyquarterly.com

Letters to the Editor

10
Reader responses to articles in *McKinsey Quarterly*, 2009 Number 2

Center Stage

84
Squeezing more ideas from product teardowns

Enduring Ideas

144
The portfolio of initiatives

In Brief

12
Why energy demand will rebound

16
Conversation Starter: **When job seekers invade Facebook**

18
Speaking of Organization: **An interview with Saad Al-Barrack**

20
Quarterly *Surveys*

22
Case in Point: **Better print and document services**

Editorial

Board of Editors
Allan R. Gold, *Editor-in-Chief*
Bill Javetski
Tom Kiely
Allen P. Webb

Senior Editors
Thomas Fleming
Lars Föyen
Roger Malone
Dennis Swinford

Associate Editors
Heather Ploog
Mary Reddy, *Information Design*
David Sims, *mckinseyquarterly.com*

***McKinsey Quarterly* Fellow**
Mrinalini Reddy

Editorial and Design Production
Donald Bergh, *Design Director*
Sue Catapano, *Managing Editor*
Roger Draper, *Copy Chief*
Drew Holzfeind, *Assistant Managing Editor*
Delilah Zak, *Associate Design Director*
Veronica Belsuzarri, *Senior Designer*
Andrew Cha, *Web Production Assistant*
Lillian Cunningham, *Editorial Assistant*

Editorial Surveys
Josselyn Simpson
Martin Rouse
Karina Lacouture

***McKinsey Quarterly* China**
Gary Chen, *Editor*
Min Ma, *Assistant Managing Editor*
Melody Xie, *Production Assistant*

Business

Jeff Pundyk, *Publisher*
Sammy Pau, *Finance*
Debra Petritsch, *Logistics*
Pamela Kelly, *Customer Service Coordinator*

Digital Media
Nicole Adams
Devin A. Brown
Jennifer Orme
Jim Santo

Web sites
mckinseyquarterly.com
china.mckinseyquarterly.com

E-mail
info@mckinseyquarterly.com

How to change your mailing address:
***McKinsey* clients via e-mail**
updates@mckinseyquarterly.com

Premium members via Web site
mckinseyquarterly.com/my_profile.aspx

McKinsey alumni via e-mail
alumni_relations@mckinsey.com

How to contact the *Quarterly*:
E-mail customer service
info@mckinseyquarterly.com

To request permission to republish an article
quarterly_reprints@mckinsey.com

To comment on an article
quarterly_comments@mckinsey.com

This Quarter

The new business of government

In the current crisis, governments around the world are taking a front-and-center role in the effort to restore financial stability and economic growth. These aims—and the local, national, and international measures needed to achieve them—rightly preoccupy government leaders.

But just as current conditions are compelling governments to play a more active role in the economy, they have also given government leaders an unprecedented opportunity to intensify their efforts to transform the way the public sector works. Many people, we know, believe that governments should now focus solely on the economic crisis. But we disagree—and not because we underestimate its seriousness. On the contrary, to address the short- and long-term economic and social challenges governments face, they must make themselves far more efficient and effective.

Many of the articles in this issue of the *Quarterly* therefore examine what the crisis means for the ways that governments operate, the role they play in the economy, and the implications for business. Our lead article, by François Bouvard, Thomas Dohrmann, and Nick Lovegrove, frames the public-sector reform imperative currently confronting government leaders around the world: why we think that now is the time to broaden, deepen, and accelerate reform, what such efforts entail, and how leaders should take reform initiatives forward. Other contributions examine the intersection of business and government: the challenges and opportunities the US economic-stimulus package creates for business, the future regulation of financial institutions, and the need for business executives to recognize and address the anger of legislators, regulators, and the public.

The imperative of government reform is a pressing and global one whose managerial and leadership challenges are as great as any in the private sector. Likewise, the growing role of government in the economy will lead to wide-ranging consequences for private enterprise. We hope that our articles provide a helpful guide for thinking about and dealing with these major issues.

Nancy Killefer
Director, Washington, DC

On Our Web Site
Now available on mckinseyquarterly.com

Conversation starters

These short essays by leading thinkers in their fields, within and outside of McKinsey, are designed to encourage discussion. Read what people are saying, then join the conversation.

Recent conversation starter:

'Power curves': What natural and economic disasters have in common

Parallels between the failures of man-made systems, such as the economy, and of similarly complex natural ones offer fascinating food for thought.

Follow us on Twitter

Receive notification of new articles by following @McKQuarterly on Twitter.

Put our widget on your page

Our widget allows you to share our latest *Quarterly* headlines on your social network, blog, or personalized page.

Videos and interactives

Exploring global energy demand

An interactive graphic examines the growth of global energy and petroleum demand based on scenarios accounting for GDP and other factors, including the potential reduction in demand through increased energy productivity.

China's 'sticky floor'

Economic success in China will hinge on fixing gender inequality.

Good boss, bad times

Management expert Robert Sutton shares lessons on handling layoffs and teams in crisis.

On Our Web Site

Join the conversation on What Matters

McKinsey's newest site convenes leading thinkers from around the world, weighing in with scores of essays on topics—from geopolitics to the credit crisis to health care—that will shape our future. Find out what matters, then join the conversation.

whatmatters.mckinseydigital.com

Find us on iTunes

McKinsey Quarterly podcasts, including conversations with authors and readings of articles, are available on iTunes.

mckinseyquarterly.com/itunes

Recent podcast:

Management lessons from the financial crisis: A conversation with Lowell Bryan and Richard Rumelt

Two business strategists discuss the nature of risk, the effectiveness of performance-measurement systems, and the difficulty of getting governance and incentives right.

Surveys

Economic Conditions Snapshot, June 2009: McKinsey Global Survey Results

Executives have become notably more optimistic about their companies' and their countries' economic prospects since mid-April—but the outlook was so poor then that optimism must be tempered.

Articles

China's green opportunity

China can and must achieve sustainable growth. Although the country has already charted an ambitious course to improve its energy efficiency and environment, a McKinsey study finds opportunities to do even more.

Where IT infrastructure and business strategy meet

CIOs and CTOs should take the lead in explaining how IT infrastructure creates business value—especially in challenging times.

The role of emotions in buying health insurance

As consumers face more choice, complexity, and financial exposure for their health care in an increasingly uncertain world, what they are really seeking is peace of mind.

Understanding online shoppers in Europe

Shopping attitudes vary across Europe. Retailers must tailor their online offers to the needs of target segments.

Helping US consumers rethink retirement

The economic crisis has left US consumers anxious and less prepared than ever for retirement, yet few are changing course.

Join the *McKinsey Quarterly* community on Facebook.

Letters to the Editor

Reader responses to articles in *McKinsey Quarterly* 2009 Number 2

Where innovation creates value

It doesn't matter where scientific discoveries and breakthrough technologies originate—for national prosperity, the important thing is who commercializes them. The United States is not behind in that race.

Having lived in Germany and seeing those picturesque shops—and having been especially frustrated to see them closed on Sundays, which was the only day I had time to do my shopping—I can appreciate Amar Bhidé's take on why American retailers might have absorbed German inventory-reduction technologies better. I've always believed that a good go-to-market strategy is what separates a great idea from blockbuster revenues, so I totally agree with Bhidé that the US is way ahead on that count.

But, my views deviate when it comes to the reason for all this. I don't believe it has anything to do with great teams or time (150 years), as Bhidé asserts. In my opinion, it's attitude. An average German citizen believes that it's unfair to make store employees work on Sundays or beyond 6 PM on Saturdays. That's why German shopping hours are much shorter than American ones; that's why they're inefficient. Even today, many Indians use the words 'crass' and 'commercialization' in the same sentence. It takes a recession like the present one for them to understand the importance of things like commercialization and go-to-market strategy.

In India and many other parts of the world, invention for the sake of invention is considered noble, whereas profiting from it is seen as greed. It's this attitude in many countries outside the US that explains America's lead in productivity and usage of innovation. This lead will be challenged severely if India and some of these other countries lose this attitude—that could take even more than 150 years. But, if India could build a mobile-phone network for close to 300 million subscribers in less than 20 years, why should it take 150 years to start putting innovation to use?

Ketharaman Swaminathan
Head of global business development, *Oracle Financial Services Software*
India

Without a doubt this is an interesting topic which has created a lively debate. Living in a country that is extremely dependent on trade with the US, what I worry about is that the commercialization of technology, for which the US is deservedly praised, will become irrelevant because it will be targeting a market with dwindling buying power (namely, the US and EMEA) while paying too little attention to the areas of emerging demand, particularly China and India. This won't happen overnight, but we could be living through the tipping point. We only have to look at the emergence of Lenovo and Huawei in China and of Tata and Mittal in India to see the emergence of commercialization innovation in these countries.

What I worry most about articles such as Amar Bhidé's is that it will lull the West into a state of self-congratulatory complacency just when it should be developing strategies to compete effectively at all levels of the innovation continuum.

Trevor Miles
Director of product marketing, *Kinaxis*
Ottawa, ON Canada

The irrational side of change management

Most change programs fail, but the odds of success can be greatly improved by taking into account these counterintuitive insights about how employees interpret their environment and choose to act.

It has been interesting to see how companies have moved from a mechanical approach to change programs toward an organizational culture where the changes are part of their "normal operational mode." What was once a recipe for a winning change program in the year 2000 is not enough in today's world. In this macroculture, competing internal change programs fail too often because they concentrate on defining better-burning platform messages (a corporate view) and they forget personal-level messaging. What has become more and more relevant is to touch people's minds and hearts. Motivating people is therefore essential.

Timo Helosuo
Director of strategy and business,
Nokia
White Plains, NY USA

The one tension that is not directly addressed in this article is between the followers' need to be led versus their need to be heard. In several situations, people actually prefer being told what to do rather than to work it out for themselves. And in my experience, they will admit this if the relationship is sufficiently strong and open.

Ashish Deo
Commercial development director of global procurement, *Diageo PLC*
London, UK

More letters from our readers on these and other articles are available on mckinseyquarterly.com.

In Brief
Research and perspectives on management

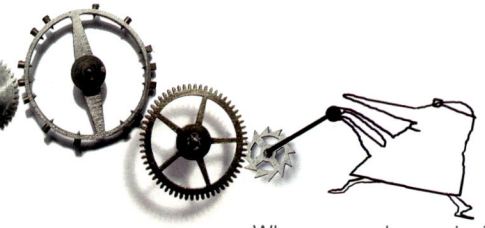

Why energy demand will rebound **12**
When job seekers invade Facebook **16**
Speaking of Organization: An interview with Saad Al-Barrak **18**
Quarterly *Surveys* **20**
Case in Point: Better print and document services **22**

Why energy demand will rebound

Scott S. Nyquist and Jaeson Rosenfeld

Scott Nyquist is a director in McKinsey's Houston office; **Jaeson Rosenfeld** is an alumnus of the Boston office and an adviser to the McKinsey Global Institute.

As the global downturn continues, the world economy faces a period of lower oil prices and overall demand for energy, a welcome change for consumers after the price spikes of recent years. But unless policy makers can find ways to improve the balance between energy supply and demand, the current slackness in energy markets will last no longer than it takes for the global economy to recover. That scenario will eventually impose significant costs on consumers and businesses in the form of higher energy prices. The importance of achieving a supply–demand balance extends, of course, beyond the next few years: in the longer term, demand seems set for robust growth.

As of late April 2009, the price of oil stood at around $50 a barrel[1] — down from a high of nearly $150 a barrel in July 2008, though many observers doubt that oil demand will rebound enough after the current economic downturn to prompt another price shock. However, research from the McKinsey Global Institute conducted in 2008 and 2009 reveals the potential for a new spike in the price of oil between 2010 and 2013. Exactly when this potential spike will occur—or if overall demand for energy will reach levels significantly above those of the pre-crisis period—depends on the length of the economic downturn.

In terms of basic market forces, it's well known that demand for oil reacts strongly to GDP levels. Sectors such as maritime shipping, trucking, petrochemicals, and air travel not only consume petroleum products heavily but also tend to overrespond to GDP downturns. On the supply side, the longer the downturn lasts and credit markets remain tight, the more high-cost supply projects will be delayed or shelved altogether. Projects nearing completion between 2009 and 2010 will be finished, but that will not ensure sufficient supply, according to our research, since marginal projects slated for startup in 2011 and beyond will be delayed, at least temporarily.

What does this mean for oil markets? For starters, the tight demand–supply balance seen at the end of 2007 could return sooner than many observers might have anticipated. A spike in the price of oil could occur as soon as 2010 under the International Monetary Fund's (IMF) "moderate" downturn scenario, which assumes a 4.7 percent GDP gap to trend with growth falling mostly in 2008 and 2009, followed by recovery in 2010. Under a "very severe" downturn scenario (which assumes a gap to trend of 10.8 percent), the time when spare capacity returns to the tighter levels of 2007 (2.5 million barrels a day) could be delayed until 2013, causing a potential price spike (Exhibit 1).

Observers who doubt that a new oil shock will occur when the economy recovers refer to the period that followed the second oil crisis in the 1970s, when demand for oil grew

Exhibit 1

Back to the future

Short-term GDP growth scenarios, million barrels of oil per day[1]

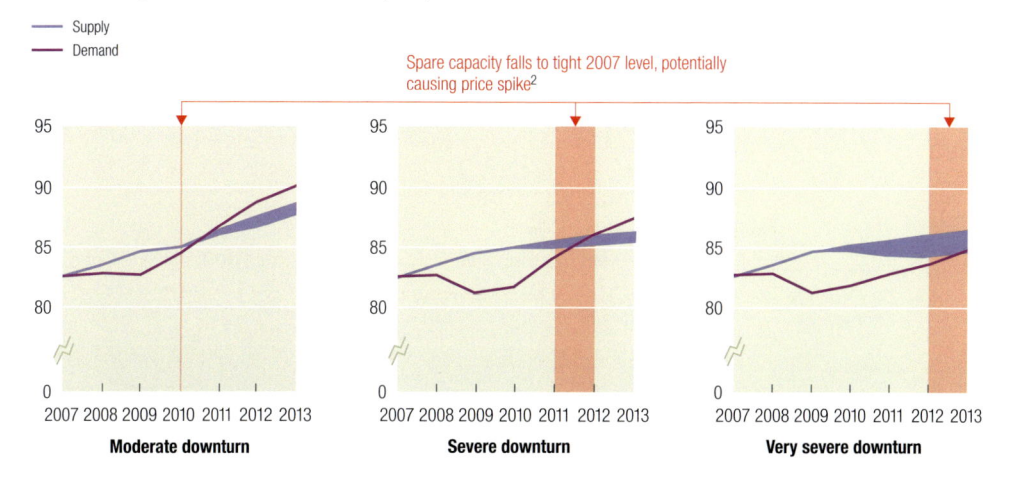

— Supply
— Demand

Spare capacity falls to tight 2007 level, potentially causing price spike[2]

Moderate downturn   **Severe downturn**   **Very severe downturn**

[1] Crude oil at the well head; includes biofuels and excludes refinery gains.
[2] 2007 level = 2.5 million barrels of oil per day.

Source: Global Insight; International Monetary Fund (IMF); McKinsey analysis

slowly for nearly two decades. However, the substitution of other products for petroleum-based ones in, for example, power generation and heating played a key role in mitigating demand in the 1980s. There are still significant low-cost opportunities on the table to replace oil with other energy sources: an estimated 8 million barrels per day of potential to boost energy efficiency and another 8 million barrels per day available from substituting petroleum products for natural gas. It is vital that these opportunities are captured, particularly given that there is a higher share of overall energy demand in some countries and regions—most notably in China, India, and the Middle East, whose economies are still rapidly increasing their levels of petroleum consumption. There are significant political hurdles to capturing this potential, but without further action to abate growing demand, a new oil shock seems inevitable.

In the long term, our research suggests continued rapid growth in overall demand for energy, further boosting the importance of efficiency efforts. From 2010 to 2020, assuming a moderate GDP downturn scenario, demand for energy will grow by 2.3 percent a year, nearly a full percentage point more than projections for 2006 to 2010. More than 90 percent of this demand expansion will come from developing

Exhibit 2

Energy demand grows in developing countries

Projected change in energy demand, moderate downturn scenario, 2010–20

≥5 quadrillion British thermal units (QBTUs)   <5 – ≥2 QBTUs   <2 QBTUs but positive demand   Negative demand

		Developing					Developed			
		Rest of world	Russia	India	China	Middle East	Japan	Northwest Europe	United States	Total
Consumer	Light-duty vehicles	5.5	0.8	2.3	4.8	2.4	−0.5	−0.5	−1.8	**13.0**
	Medium and heavy trucks	3.3	0.2	1.0	1.7	0.9	−0.1	0.4	0.6	**8.0**
	Air transport	2.2	0.3	0.0	0.9	0.4	0.3	0.9	0.7	**5.7**
	Residential	14.9	0.7	3.2	11.6	4.6	0.0	1.7	1.5	**38.2**
	Commercial	3.3	0.9	1.4	5.5	0.5	1.1	0.8	1.7	**15.3**
Industrial	Steel	3.6	−0.1	3.7	9.7	0.2	−0.5	−0.1	0.1	**16.6**
	Petrochemicals	4.1	0.9	1.3	8.8	3.3	0.0	1.0	1.4	**20.8**
	Pulp and paper	0.6	0.4	0.1	0.8	0.0	−0.3	0.2	−0.8	**1.0**
	Refining	0.1	0.1	0.4	0.4	0.6	−0.1	−0.5	−0.5	**0.5**
	Other industrial	20.7	−0.3	1.1	8.2	5.0	0.5	1.4	2.9	**39.5**
	Total	**58.3**	**3.9**	**14.5**	**52.4**	**17.9**	**0.4**	**5.3**	**5.8**	**158.5**

Source: International Energy Agency; McKinsey analysis

regions, with China, India, and the Middle East leading the way. Five sectors within China—residential and commercial buildings, steel, petrochemicals, and light vehicles—will account for more than 25 percent of global energy demand growth. India's light-vehicle, residential-buildings, and steel sectors and the Middle East's light-vehicle and petrochemicals sectors will be other notable contributors to the growing demand for energy (Exhibit 2).

In contrast, we estimate that growth in energy demand will be virtually flat in Japan, as well as in the United States, where demand for fossil fuels will remain largely unchanged until 2020 and overall energy demand will grow at 0.4 percent per year. Europe, however, will see the rate of growth increase to around 1 percent, reflecting higher economic growth in the developing countries of Central and Eastern Europe. Several sectors in developed economies will see energy demand contract. Most notable are the light-vehicle sector, where energy-efficiency regulations are leading to a dramatic slowdown in energy demand, and the pulp and paper sector, where demand is shrinking as a result of a shift from paper to digital media.

If policy makers act to head off a potential price shock—in response to a renewed imbalance in energy markets—there is considerable potential on the demand side (the focus of this research) as well as on the supply side. By 2020, we estimate that growth in demand for oil could fall by 6 million to 11 million barrels a day, which would probably balance demand and supply within this period. The available policy levers, which could be used at reasonable cost to make this happen, include incentives to shift petroleum out of boiler-fuel applications, mostly into natural gas; the removal of subsidies for petroleum products; and further incentives to raise fuel efficiency. To avoid an oil shock in a 2010 to 2013 time frame, policy makers would need to ramp up fuel-efficiency standards in developing countries rapidly while actively working to remove subsidies and create incentives for substitution.

Regulatory action to increase the productivity of all sources of energy—the output achieved for a given level of energy consumed—could abate the projected 2020 demand by between 16 and 20 percent. This could cut energy demand growth from now until 2020 by two-thirds or more. Heating and cooling buildings more efficiently, for example, presents significant opportunity for reducing energy demand, though this will require establishing and enforcing strong building standards. Developing countries represent most of the potential savings, partly because between now and 2020 they will install half or more of the capital stock that will be in place in the latter year, and the economics of better heating and cooling technologies are more attractive in new buildings than in old ones.

Lower oil prices and overall demand for energy because of the economic downturn are a temporary blessing that should not lull policy makers and businesses into a false sense of complacency. Given our projections, it is essential that they step up their efforts now to secure that energy is used in more efficient ways. o

[1] As of publication, oil prices were approximately $70 a barrel.

Conversation Starter

Short essays by leading thinkers on management topics

When job seekers invade Facebook

Soumitra Dutta and Matthew Fraser

As the downturn continues, millions of corporate managers—gripped by the job jitters—are rushing to join online social networks in a scramble to build their social capital. The popularity of sites such as LinkedIn is soaring: less than a year ago the site had little brand profile and was seen mostly as a venue for corporate suits trolling for professional contacts while plotting their next career move. Facebook, by contrast, has largely attracted individuals seeking a compelling site for fun social networking.

Today LinkedIn's year-on-year growth is up nearly 200 percent in the United States and it now has more than 35 million members—many of whom were formerly employed within the hard-hit financial sector. And it's just one of the many sites to which recession-struck managers are flocking: Xing (based in Germany), with its 7 million members and special Lehman Brothers alumni section, and Meet the Boss (based in the United Kingdom), which restricts membership to C-level financial types, are also experiencing burgeoning membership levels.

This surging popularity of online social networking is transforming the nature of business networking, with profound implications for the way business people manage their careers. But it also augurs profound change for social networking itself.

With so many people stampeding into Web-based social networks, the line between social and business networking is becoming increasingly blurred. An important question is whether the values and codes of conduct specific to the virtual world will come into conflict with real-world values and norms. Facebook, where the idea of a "friend" is directly embedded in the interface, is increasingly cluttered with self-promoters, career artists, and marketing entrepreneurs. What happens as this trend intensifies and those using Facebook exclusively for career networking invade?

There are, of course, powerful economic reasons behind the trend. As sociologist Nan Lin puts it in his book *Social Capital*,[1] "Individuals engage in interactions and networking in order to produce profits." These profits are based upon information, influence, social credentials, and recognition. The accumulated social capital, meanwhile, helps individuals to gain competitive advantages in the labor market as a result of privileged access to "resources" located on the social networks.

[1] Nan Lin, *Social Capital: A Theory of Social Structure and Action*, New York: Cambridge University Press, 2001.

Professor Soumitra Dutta is Roland Berger Chaired Professor of Business and Technology, and **Dr. Matthew Fraser** is a senior research fellow at INSEAD.

Still, for many there's nothing more irritating than when a new "friend" contacts you almost immediately with an inappropriate request for a favor. Generally, it's more advisable to approach social networking as a giver, not a taker, and gradually build relationships according to reciprocated favors. Overall, online social networking, with its support groups and trusted access, is governed by a culture of sharing, not selling.

And can the throngs of interlopers really be considered friends? Anthropologists tell us that it's impossible to maintain stable social relationships with more than 150 people. Maintaining a professional network of more than 150 looser connections on LinkedIn might be plausible, but it would strain the richer social relations that make up the fabric of sites such as Facebook. Among Facebook's more than 200 million members, the instances of "defriending" are already growing.

It's a safe bet that if the economic downturn grinds on, we will witness further conflict between the nonrational instinct to connect socially and the rational calculation to build social capital for professional reasons. If so, it may put further strain on the notion of an online friend. We may find ourselves asking more frequently that age-old question, "What are friends for?" o

> *The 'newness' of this particular mode of communication speeds up the process of social networking; but it doesn't change it. It is still human driven. True, some people will be better at it than others, just as some abusers will be better at abusing than others.*
> —Richard Eastman

> *The sooner companies and executives 'get with the program' of 'making friends,' the better. Not because they are in a problem and now they want to 'make' friends, but because being socially active is one of the main reasons one climbs the ladder.*
> —Mohammad Khan

> *There is just no substitute for meeting a colleague, shaking hands, and either agreeing to stay in contact or moving on and tossing their business card on your way out.*
> —Zofia Dripps

Read what other people are saying at mckinseyquarterly.com, then join the conversation.

Speaking of Organization

An interview with Saad Al-Barrak

John Tiefel

Saad Al-Barrak has transformed the Kuwait-based telco Zain over the past six years from a local player into a company that serves 56 million customers in 22 Middle Eastern and African countries. Zain's global growth has been driven by Al-Barrak, better known as Dr. Saad, who became CEO in 2002. In these interview excerpts, Dr. Saad discusses his belief that too much control undermines productivity and creativity, and his management theory of "chaos by design."

The Quarterly: *Zain's corporate culture is unusual—you call it "chaos by design." What is that?*

Saad Al-Barrak: To start with, management is a human experiment, a human endeavor. It is an art, not a science. No two people in the world are identical—people are different because of their experiences, beliefs, vision, whatever. And so every human organization is unique, and this complexity and diversity of people multiplies when more people join an organization.

Also, traditional management styles and structures have a big problem at their root: if you try to make management a science, then you will treat people as machines and produce a machine bureaucracy, which stifles innovation. If you subject people to this grinding mill of a machine, you are downgrading their intellectual capacity to that of animals. After all, that's what you do with animals performing in a circus: you train them to do certain things—best practices—and they come and perform in front of people. The expectations for them are very consistent, and they take pride in meeting those very consistent expectations.

That's the management circus, which we at Zain are not willing to accept. Therefore, the whole point here is to design our systems, set up our structures, and conduct our business with values and principles as our only guide. Beyond that, the sky is the limit—everything is subject to a fresh look and a fresh perspective. We will infinitely adapt to our dynamically changing conditions and resources.

For example, I have recruited many people regardless of whether there was a place for them in our organizational structure. Different people with new, fresh perspectives are always joining us. And if they are the right people to work with us, we create new positions for them and amend our organization accordingly. After all, you cannot design systems without thoroughly considering your input.

The Quarterly: *Does this constant change make it difficult to manage ongoing operations?*

John Tiefel is a director in McKinsey's Dubai office.

'Everything is subject to a fresh look and a fresh perspective'

Saad Al-Barrak
CEO, Zain

Saad Al-Barrak: Continually changing very quickly might seem like virtual chaos, but for me it's the ultimate in organization. In today's world, change is rapid. If we were too bound by processes, we would not have the passion that drives performance in our company. We would not be able to respond quickly to a changing environment, because the systems and processes would fight back. That's a handicap of the old, overorganized organizational paradigm.

The *Quarterly*: *Can you tell us more about how you encourage passion among your employees, old and new?*

Saad Al-Barrak: First, we take pride in contributing to the development of societies, in many ways, through mobile telecommunication. That is our greatest passion.

Communication is the most critical human activity. And though technology enables communication, technology alone can't create success or passion. Given the market's competitiveness, branding and marketing come into play now at much higher levels than they did before.

Our ultimate aim is to become the "sweetheart" of any community we work with, not a business trying to take advantage of a community—selling products and services for a premium, taking a lot of money, and so on. In fact, we don't want pricing to become an issue at all. We want people to feel happy about buying our services because they attach great value to association with our company. They feel passionate toward you because you represent a great vehicle to take society forward.

If you think this is fuzzy and I'm talking generalities, no! That kind of passion matters inside the company too. Set up an organization that makes people feel rich in every direction—financially, intellectually, in terms of knowledge and expertise—because they feel sure that it is a great and fair organization and feel pride in being associated with it and its contribution to the community. That is an organization people would love to be recruited by.

And you can achieve that only through the kind of management philosophy I described. You cannot do it through old books on shelves. You don't teach this art—you live it. It's group learning, it's dialogue, it's a strategic conversation that you take forward. We talk about the need to ignite the passion of people to the maximum in order to get the best out of them. That's how you do it. It's not something to lecture about; it is something to live and embody.

Quarterly Surveys

Selected results from surveys of the *Quarterly*'s online readers and panel of global executives

Governance in the crisis

Many boards of directors are not providing the leadership demanded by the global economic crisis. While half of board members describe their boards as effective in managing the crisis, just over a third say their boards have not been effective; 14 percent aren't sure how to rate their boards' performance. At the personal level, roughly half of corporate directors say their boards' chairs haven't met the demands of the crisis, and a nearly equal percentage of board chairs believe the same about their board members.

Most boards have nevertheless responded to the crisis by making some procedural changes, such as thoroughly discussing how the crisis affects fundamental strategic assumptions and ensuring that a wider range of information about the company is presented at meetings. Further, among directors at companies that have already changed their procedures in some way, 62 percent say their boards should continue to change. The results indicate that directors are willing to shake up board procedures by inviting new participants—including outsiders—to participate in meetings or by increasing board members' firsthand experience of the crisis—for example, with visits to customers or distributors.

From "A lack of leadership: A McKinsey survey of corporate directors," February 2009, which received responses from 186 corporate directors.

Boards' procedural changes in context of the global economic turmoil, % of respondents[1]

- Changes made since global economic turmoil began,[1] n = 186
- Additional changes board should make to become more effective in managing the global economic crisis,[2] n = 152

	Changes made	Additional changes
Openly and thoroughly discussing how the crisis affects fundamental strategic assumptions	47	30
Ensuring that a wider range of detailed information about our company is presented at meetings	30	21
Ensuring that a wider range of detailed information about our industry is presented at meetings	19	32
Including new participants in meetings	18	32
Increasing board members' firsthand experience of the crisis (eg, visiting customers/distributors)	7	28

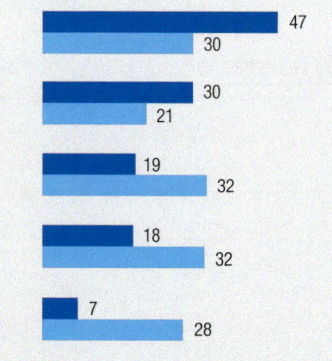

[1] Respondents who answered "other" or "don't know" are not shown.
[2] Includes respondents who have made changes since global economic turmoil began.

In Brief

Management in the crisis

Many executives say their corporate-management teams are doing a good job in the crisis. Indeed, more than half of all respondents—57 percent—say that because of good management, their companies have been less hurt than most by the crisis. Although that figure probably indicates hope for better results than are entirely plausible, it also indicates a confidence in management that runs counter to many other reports. Indeed, even at companies where executives expect profits to drop in the first half of 2009, 51 percent say that their companies have been well managed, along with 52 percent of executives at financial firms.

What's interesting, companies that (according to their executives) are well managed have a focus somewhat different from the one that executives at poorly managed companies support. Well-managed companies have a much stronger emphasis on reducing both operating costs and capital spending, as well as on improving productivity. Although executives at poorly managed companies also advocate cutting operating costs, they then turn to restructuring and hiring.

From "Economic Conditions Snapshot, March 2009: McKinsey Global Survey Results," which includes the responses of 1,630 executives from around the world.

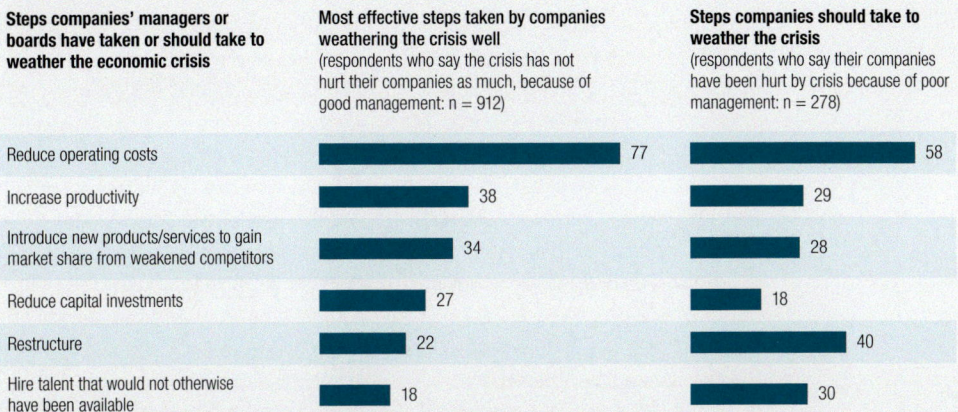

% of respondents[1]

Steps companies' managers or boards have taken or should take to weather the economic crisis	Most effective steps taken by companies weathering the crisis well (respondents who say the crisis has not hurt their companies as much, because of good management: n = 912)	Steps companies should take to weather the crisis (respondents who say their companies have been hurt by crisis because of poor management: n = 278)
Reduce operating costs	77	58
Increase productivity	38	29
Introduce new products/services to gain market share from weakened competitors	34	28
Reduce capital investments	27	18
Restructure	22	40
Hire talent that would not otherwise have been available	18	30

[1]Respondents who answered "don't know" are not shown.

The full results of these surveys are available on mckinseyquarterly.com/surveys.

Case in Point

Better print and document services:
A hidden source of value

Ferruccio Lagutaine and Stefano Martinotti

Situation
Managing the flow of documents is an immense, complex, and critical task for many sectors, particularly financial services, government, long-distance marketing, and publishing. The rising tide includes printed and electronic documents sent to customers (bills, marketing brochures) and those received from them (insurance claims, changes in personal information), as well as internal documents for employees.

Most organizations handle documents in scattered units that manage both output services (the design, composition, and production of documents for physical and electronic distribution) and input services (receiving, sorting, and storing incoming documents). A typical global financial institution might spend 0.5 percent of its revenues on print and document services—a significant sum.

Recently, a big insurance company looking for savings to finance growth decided to target document operations. Spending was high and evidence of waste widespread. In some locations, under a third of all marketing brochures reached designated customers.

Top executives thought an integrated document-management strategy could cut costs and improve operations significantly. Analysis revealed that over three years these costs might fall by up to €150 million—a third of the total.

Complication
The company faced a major obstacle: document service units, each with a different operating model, were dispersed across 30-plus nations. Several local executives, worrying that the centralization of print and document services would diminish the agility and quality of local marketing, disliked relinquishing control over a function that directly touched important customers.

Resolution
The company established a document advisory function with end-to-end responsibility for all document processes: printing, composition, archiving, and supplier management, as well as traditional and electronic distribution. The broader mission was to manage demand for documents more effectively, ensure that designs followed cost guidelines, standardize processes, promote electronic distribution, and establish more individualized marketing communications.

This advisory function established national teams that included people with skills in art and design (and a willingness to follow new corporate norms), IT processes and tools, and basic management and leadership. While these teams reported to the local COO, the corporate center

Ferruccio Lagutaine is a principal in McKinsey's Zurich office, where **Stefano Martinotti** is a consultant.

Exhibit

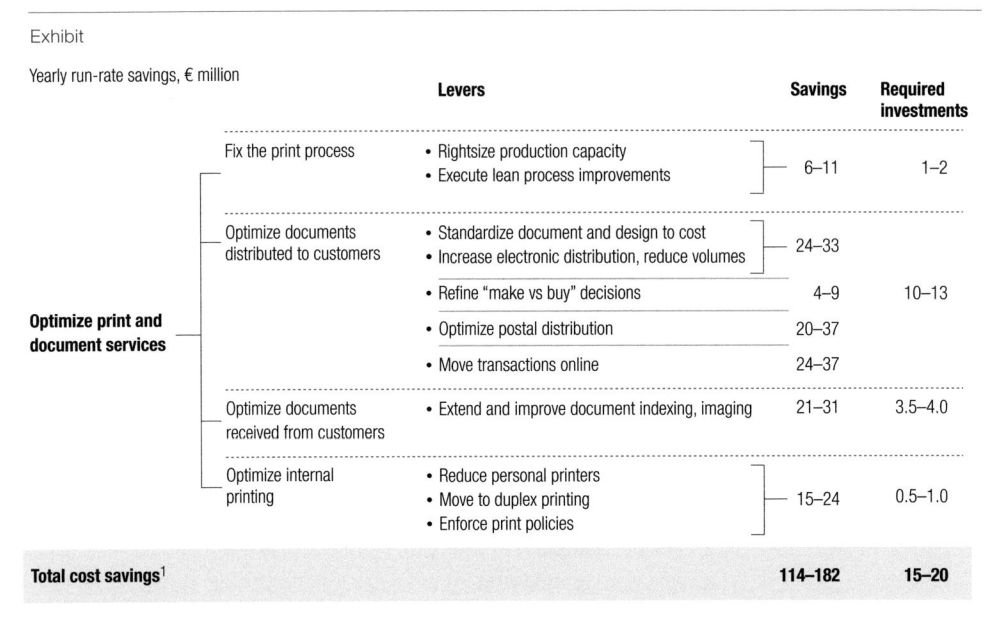

Yearly run-rate savings, € million

	Levers	Savings	Required investments
Optimize print and document services			
Fix the print process	• Rightsize production capacity • Execute lean process improvements	6–11	1–2
Optimize documents distributed to customers	• Standardize document and design to cost • Increase electronic distribution, reduce volumes	24–33	10–13
	• Refine "make vs buy" decisions	4–9	
	• Optimize postal distribution	20–37	
	• Move transactions online	24–37	
Optimize documents received from customers	• Extend and improve document indexing, imaging	21–31	3.5–4.0
Optimize internal printing	• Reduce personal printers • Move to duplex printing • Enforce print policies	15–24	0.5–1.0
Total cost savings[1]		**114–182**	**15–20**

[1] Approximately 25% of total cost savings are subject to potential social constraints mainly related to optimization of document input services (eg, rightsizing of workforce dedicated to reception, distribution of incoming documents); total required investment consists primarily of project costs (eg, process reengineering, change management) and, to a lesser extent, IT costs (eg, an e-procurement tool).

set their incentives and goals. A leader of each team served on the group's governance body and was responsible for sharing knowledge and promoting best practices. Just by following a directive to standardize the weight and format of paper for client communications, one country operation cut production costs by 10 percent.

The local structure helped mitigate the concerns of country executives who feared ceding too much control. Higher-level coordination and goal setting enabled the company to standardize practices and realize broad economies, so it achieved its cost reduction target of €150 million in three years. And since the company relied on managerial and organizational initiatives, the new approach required investments of only €15 million.

Implications

An integrated document services strategy can realize significant savings for many organizations in a wide spectrum of industries (exhibit). In today's environment, it will suit many companies looking for significant cost reductions but under pressure to minimize investments. Additionally, branding is more effective when companies standardize marketing's look and language. US customer communications in financial services are highly regulated, so better document management may reduce compliance risks too.

Organizations can also improve the customer experience by using document services to individualize communications. And one company, acting on the advisory function's advice, attached marketing communications to its clients' transaction documents. By reducing paper consumption and increasing electronic communications, the company met its customer commitments while "greening" operations.

26
The new normal

29
The case for government reform now

39
Reforming the public sector in a crisis:
An interview with Sweden's former prime minister

47
New challenges for Asia's governments

Special report: Inside the US stimulus program

50
Introduction: Implications for three industries

53
Energy: Investing in efficiency

56
Health care: Taking medical records online

59
Broadband: Improving access

61
Weighing the US government's response to the crisis: A dialogue

68
Learning from financial regulation's mistakes

75
Rebuilding corporate reputations

Government and business:
New rules for a new era

Artwork by David Senior

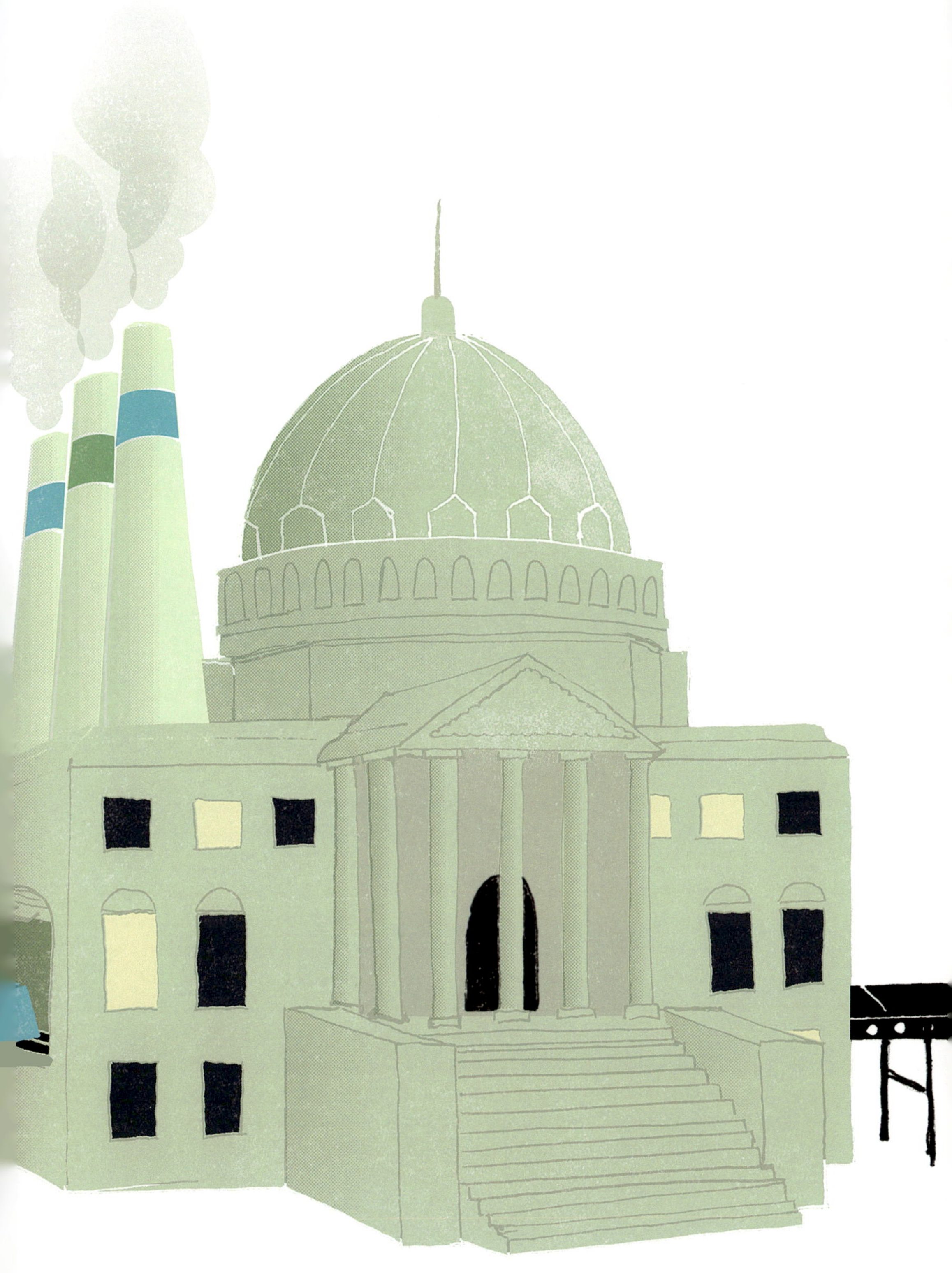

The new normal

The business landscape has changed fundamentally; tomorrow's environment will be different, but no less rich in possibilities for those who are prepared.

Ian Davis

Ian Davis is a senior partner in McKinsey's London office.

It is increasingly clear that the current downturn is fundamentally different from recessions of recent decades. We are experiencing not merely another turn of the business cycle, but a restructuring of the economic order.

For some organizations, near-term survival is the only agenda item. Others are peering through the fog of uncertainty, thinking about how to position themselves once the crisis has passed and things return to normal. The question is, "What will normal look like?" While no one can say how long the crisis will last, what we find on the other side will not look like the normal of recent years. The new normal will be shaped by a confluence of powerful forces—some arising directly from the financial crisis and some that were at work long before it began.

Obviously, there will be significantly less financial leverage in the system. But it is important to realize that the rise in leverage leading up to the crisis had two sources. The first was a legitimate increase in debt due to financial innovation—new instruments and ways of doing business that reduced risk and added value to the economy. The second was a credit bubble fueled by misaligned incentives, irresponsible risk taking, lax oversight, and fraud. Where the former ends and the latter begins is the multitrillion dollar question, but it is clear that the future will reveal significantly lower levels of leverage (and higher prices for risk) than we had come to expect. Business models that rely on high leverage will suffer reduced returns. Companies that boost returns to equity the old fashioned way—through real productivity gains—will be rewarded.

Another defining feature of the new normal will be an expanded role for government. In the 1930s, during the Great Depression, the Roosevelt administration permanently redefined the role of government in the US financial system. All signs point to an equally significant regulatory restructuring to come. Some will welcome this, on the grounds that modernization of the regulatory system was clearly overdue. Others will view the changes as unwanted political interference. Either way, the reality is that around the world governments will be calling the shots in sectors (such as debt insurance) that were once only lightly regulated. They will also be demanding new levels of transparency and disclosure for investment vehicles such as hedge funds and getting involved in decisions that were once the sole province of corporate boards, including executive compensation.

While the financial-services industry will be most directly affected, the impact of government's increased role will be widespread: there is a risk of a new era of financial protectionism. A good outcome of the crisis would be greater global financial coordination and transparency. A bad outcome would be protectionist policies that make it harder for companies to move capital to the most productive places and that dampen economic growth, particularly in the developing world. Companies need to prepare for such an eventuality—even as they work to avert it.

These two forces—less leverage and more government—arise directly from the financial crisis, but there are others that were already at work and that have been strengthened by recent events. For example, it was clear before the crisis began that US consumption could not continue to be the engine for global growth. Consumption depends on income growth, and US income growth since 1985 had been boosted by a series of one-time factors—such as the entry of women into the workforce, an increase in the number of college graduates—that have now played themselves out. Moreover, although the peak spending years of the baby boom generation helped boost consumption in the '80s and '90s, as boomers age and begin to live off of retirement savings that were too small even before housing and stock market wealth evaporated, consumption levels will fall.

Companies seeking high rates of income and consumption growth will increasingly look to Asia. The fundamental drivers of Asian growth— productivity gains, technology adoption, and cultural and institutional changes—did not halt as a result of the 1997 Asian financial crisis. And Asian economies—though they have rapidly deteriorated in recent months—are unlikely to be stopped by this one. The big unknown is whether the temptation to blame Western-style capitalism for current troubles will lead to backlash and self-destructive policies. If this can be avoided, the world's economic center of gravity will continue to shift eastward.

Related articles on mckinseyquarterly.com
Leading through uncertainty
Strategy in a 'structural break'
A better way to fix the banks

Through it all, technological innovation will continue, and the value of increasing human knowledge will remain undiminished. For talented contrarians and technologists, the next few years may prove especially fruitful as investors looking for high-risk, high-reward opportunities shift their attention from financial engineering to genetic engineering, software, and clean energy.

Copyright © 2009 McKinsey & Company. All rights reserved.

We welcome your comments on this article. Please send them to quarterly_comments@mckinsey.com.

This much is certain: when we finally enter into the post-crisis period, the business and economic context will not have returned to its pre-crisis state. Executives preparing their organizations to succeed in the new normal must focus on what has changed and what remains basically the same for their customers, companies, and industries. The result will be an environment that, while different from the past, is no less rich in possibilities for those who are prepared. o

The case for government reform now

The expanded role of governments means that taxpayers will pay more for public services—and will demand more in return. To meet these expectations, the public sector must transform itself.

François Bouvard, Thomas Dohrmann, and Nick Lovegrove

François Bouvard is a director in McKinsey's Paris office; **Thomas Dohrmann** is a principal in the Washington, DC, office, where **Nick Lovegrove** is a director.

Long before governments around the world faced the current economic crisis, they wrestled with many difficult, complex challenges—health care, social security, education, national security, crime, and critical infrastructure. The demands on public services were growing, along with the burden on taxpayers, and there was no long-term certainty about how to pay the bill. Several countries ran large budget deficits, raising already high levels of public debt.

In recent months, the pressures on governments have multiplied further as a result of a potent cocktail of interlocking emergencies—the financial and economic crises, major shifts in energy prices, climate change, food supplies, and natural resources. The combined effects threaten economic and social breakdown as consumers suffer and unemployment and poverty rise. Even the viability of capitalism has been questioned.

Whatever the public sector's role has been in creating these crises, few doubt that it has a critical role in resolving them. Governments are not only intervening to an unprecedented degree in private markets—to rescue or reinforce banks, insurance companies, and automobile manufacturers, among others—but also accumulating financial covenants that threaten their long-term solvency in the process. Indeed, at a time when they have limited political, social, and financial room for maneuver, they are taking on a whole range of tasks beyond the scope of traditional policy and public services.

So now more than ever, governments must discharge their functions efficiently and effectively. But few of them have an established track record or reputation for managerial excellence. Indeed, their historical performance running departments and agencies often arouses skepticism. Many public officials, knowing this, seek to reform the way government works.

In our experience, these reforms typically fall short: with few exceptions, they skim the surface, cover too little ground, take too long, and leave much of the public sector relatively untouched. That's why we see a need for broader, deeper, and faster reform: what we call whole-government transformation. The current crisis provides both the necessity and the chance to improve the machinery of the state fundamentally—a challenge of vast scale and urgency.

There are relatively few instances of governments taking an integrated approach to reform, but those few illustrate the scale of the opportunity, especially for raising productivity. Under the prime ministership of Göran Persson, for instance, Sweden's government responded to its mid-1990s budget crisis by shaving 11 percent from operational budgets, with no apparent damage to performance, and then maintained tight control over future spending (see "Reforming the public sector in a crisis: An interview with Sweden's former prime minister," in this section). In 2004, Tony Blair announced the "Gershon targets"—led by Peter Gershon, then head of the Office of Government Commerce—which generated £26.5 billion a year in improved efficiencies. In November 2008, the UK government announced plans to save an additional £35 billion a year. Similarly, the integrated transformation program of Nicolas Sarkozy's government in France aims to cut costs by €7.7 billion as of 2012. It's important to note that the adoption and implementation of these efficiency targets have gone hand in hand with reforms focused on significant improvements in outcomes, such as higher test scores in schools and reduced waiting times in hospitals.

The size of the prize from government reform is so large that it more than justifies the enormous effort required. If the US government could achieve the 15 percent or more productivity improvement we typically expect from a major private-sector change program, for instance, the savings to taxpayers would exceed $134 billion annually (more than $445 per citizen) on 2010 federal addressable spending of approximately $900 billion.

The right time for government reform
Some people argue that governments have more than enough to do addressing the current crisis and can't afford to divert time and attention to seemingly less pressing matters like a whole-government transformation.

Nor can such a transformation be undertaken lightly. Tony Blair famously said that "I bear the scars" from one particularly grueling round of reform. Change, never easy in any large institution, always seems harder in government, whose scale and complexity are daunting. So too is the challenge of initiating reform under the close scrutiny of the public, the press, and the legislature.

It's tempting to postpone the reform of government until the crisis is resolved. Yet that would be a mistake. The crisis is actually the right time to undertake far-reaching changes.

It's a necessity
Reform is now a necessity, not a choice. As governments assume a broader, more significant role in response to the crisis, it becomes ever more important that they should be efficient and effective—otherwise, they would compound the severity of the problems. This crisis is the public sector's ultimate test.

Yet few governments are equipped to meet it, either as a whole or at the level of individual departments and agencies. Too often, we find, the fragmented silos of governments work at cross purposes. Political appointees and civil servants have different goals and mind-sets. Confidence and tolerance for risk are low. There is little willingness to question historic practices and orthodoxies or to create a performance culture focusing on quality, costs, and access. Addressing these shortcomings in the middle of a crisis might seem like trying to fix an airplane in flight—but sometimes that's needed to land it safely.

The fiscal imperative
Before the crisis, many governments were already spending well beyond their means to meet current obligations (exhibit). Aging populations and the consequent pressures on health care, social security, and pension systems were sure to compound rising budget deficits and debt service burdens. Clearly, the crisis will reduce tax revenues for the foreseeable future and require most governments to invest extraordinary amounts of money to rescue failing institutions—even whole industries—restart the flow of credit, and stimulate demand.

How will governments restore something like a long-term equilibrium to their finances? They could do so by increasing taxes—which would be unpopular with taxpayers and at least a short-term drag on economic growth—or by reducing transfer payments or other spending programs. Tax increases and budget cuts may be unavoidable in the coming years, but governments could minimize them by concentrating on raising efficiency and effectiveness, so that public spending yields the maximum benefit. In fact, improving the performance of government, though perhaps the most challenging of all available levers to implement, may be the most feasible politically. The improvement must take place across the board: uncoordinated, incremental initiatives couldn't possibly reduce the public sector's financial burden enough to meet the challenge.

The public's expectations and demands
Governments struggle to reconcile the desire for better public services with a reluctance to pay for them, and there was much dissatisfaction with their quality even in happier economic times. The increased role governments now play as a result of the crisis means that taxpayers will pay more for public services—now or later—and will expect and demand more in return.

Opportunity for reform
The idea that "a crisis is too good an opportunity to waste" is becoming commonplace. Businesses around the world are seizing this opportunity to rethink their operating assumptions and even reinvent themselves, often radically. Governments must do the same. The crisis may well mark what UCLA professor Richard Rumelt calls a "structural break from the past—a moment when many of the critical assumptions that have driven our previous behavior and attitudes no longer seem correct or appropriate."[1] It may also force the long-overdue clarification of the roles of the private and public sectors in a modern economy. For these and other reasons, we now have a once-in-a-generation opportunity to achieve a whole-government transformation.

Raising the government's game
The reform agenda will differ from country to country, but there should be important points in common. First, most governments will need to broaden their approach to reform: a dispersed, sporadic one—a single department or agency at a time—can't achieve the level of change now required. Few governments have ever adopted an integrated reform program, but most will have no choice.

Such programs should reach most if not all departments and agencies. No doubt it makes sense to focus on the largest parts of the public sector—critical, high-cost services like health care, education, and defense. Nonetheless, small and little-known corners of government can yield significant breakthroughs and serve as pioneers or pilots. A broad approach to reform is also very useful to share the burdens

---

[1] Richard P. Rumelt, "Strategy in a 'structural break,'" mckinseyquarterly.com, December 2008.

and expectations it creates, to emphasize the shared pain and gain, to generate greater peer pressure, and to reveal the comparative performance of different parts of the public sector. A deeper approach to reform will also be needed. Most reform programs in the past didn't reach down into the inner core of governments, which will now have to make fundamental changes in the way thousands—in some cases, millions—of their employees work.

Interaction and coordination among departments and agencies at the local, national, and international levels is important too. Since the silos characterizing government organizations make effective cooperation across their boundaries especially difficult, this must be a critical element of reform.

Performance management

In recent years, a number of governments have strengthened the way individual departments and agencies deliver their services and manage performance. But as we often see in the private sector, it's necessary to go further by establishing a true performance-management regime and culture across every unit. The essential elements include goals focused on outcomes, an integrated way of allocating the right quantity and quality of resources for each objective, clear accountability across agencies, accurate and consistent measurements of progress, and benchmarking against best practice. Intervention to address emerging shortfalls and tangible consequences for success and failure are important as well. The UK government, with its Public Service Agreements for each department, supported by the Prime Minister's Delivery Unit at the center, has implemented many elements of that approach. The French government is taking a similarly tough-minded one.

> Few governments have ever adopted an integrated reform program, but most will have no choice

Citizen-focused public services

Although some people take offense when governments adopt the language of business—for instance, by referring to citizens as customers—citizens in many countries clearly do want to be treated as valued customers of the public services they pay for through taxes. Pioneering governments have captured this idea's power by redesigning key public services around the people who use them, transforming their effectiveness and, sometimes, their efficiency. Service Canada, for instance, has merged more than 70 services from a number of agencies into a unified customer service organization that groups its offerings around the needs of citizens. In the process, it has saved more than CN $400 million a year through increased efficiency and accuracy.

Talent management

Most government departments and agencies are people businesses that depend on the quality and capabilities of their talent. Yet many governments already have a talent deficit, notably for frontline roles such as doctors and teachers. They also face an impending demographic time bomb of retirements that threatens to widen the deficit and undermine their institutional memory.

Several governments are therefore rediscovering the lost art of managing talent, to attract the "best and the brightest" and give these future leaders the managerial tools and methodologies they need to perform at the highest level. The United Kingdom's Professional Skills for Government program, for instance, has substantially upgraded the managerial training of senior civil servants. Niche enterprises such as Teach for America (in the United States) and Teach First (in the United Kingdom) have shown how the public sector can work with social entrepreneurs to attract distinctive talent.

The challenge is great: governments face an urgent need—but also a great opportunity—to modernize their approach to managing talent. For starters, they must rethink their employee value proposition—the reason a talented person would want to work for them—identify and implement incentives to encourage superior performance and

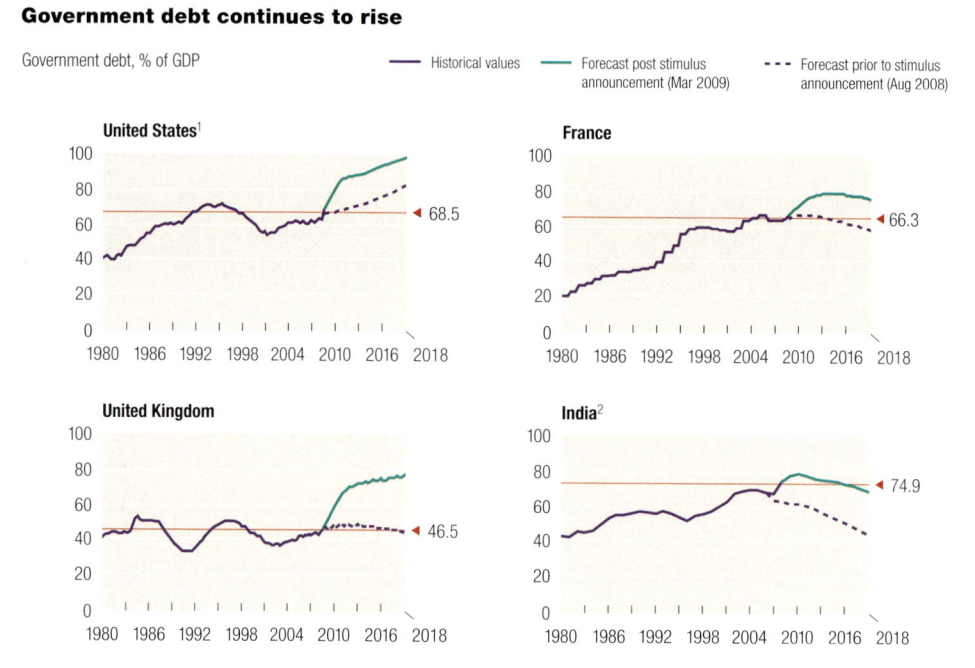

Exhibit

Government debt continues to rise

[1] Represents total debt, including debt on government accounts that the United States owes to itself.
[2] Includes federal- and state-level public debt.

Source: Oxford Economics (Aug 2008 and Mar 2009 baselines)

penalize underperformance, and establish productive, collaborative relationships with public-sector unions. The forthcoming increased rates of retirement should be used as an opportunity to renew the talent pool and establish new working models with less built-in overstaffing and redundancy.

Lean operations

Governments are starting to recognize that much of what they do is configured around large, complex service operations, often labor intensive and essentially static. Lean-operations techniques are improving the efficiency and effectiveness of some parts of the public sector—defense logistics, hospital waiting times, tax and immigration assessment processes, and even policy development, for example. The results frequently exceed expectations: one tax authority, for instance, processed 75 percent more returns while cutting assessment errors by 40 percent and processing lead times by 80 percent. As the pressures to deliver more with less grow, governments will need to deepen and intensify their use of lean techniques to transform service operations.

Spending on external goods and services will have to be managed more carefully as well. These expenditures are rising significantly, yet few governments have modernized and professionalized their procurement and contracting. For many of them, now forced to stanch the outflow of funds, this is an immediate priority. Addressing it will not only ensure that governments get better value for money but also make their suppliers more productive.

Information systems

Most governments recognize information technology's increasingly prominent role and are committed to large, ambitious IT-development programs. Several tax authorities and social-security administrations that conduct much of their business online, for instance, have dramatically improved their efficiency and service quality. But large-scale public-sector IT programs have run into costly and embarrassing difficulties—notably in important areas, such as electronic medical records.

Perhaps that's why governments tend to adopt new technology more slowly than the private sector does—indeed, more slowly than citizens in their homes do. It's hard to believe that the public sector can meet its current and future challenges if the technology gap persists. But to address it, governments must learn to manage large IT programs in a timely and cost-effective way.

Leading reform in a crisis

Government reform can and should be seen as a direct response to the economic crisis, not a distraction from it. In fact, it provides a powerful context for accelerating the pace.

Even so, there are complications. Government reform programs have a mixed track record, partly reflecting the fact that the public sector is larger and more complex than even the biggest commercial businesses. The ambiguous results also reflect the specific challenges facing governments—relatively limited capabilities and an ossified organizational culture, as well as strong political pressures that make it harder for government leaders to focus on the long-term transformation and make the tough choices it requires (see sidebar, "Why government reform is hard").

Government reform faces another challenge too: this may not be the best time to raise productivity by cutting public employment substantially. With rising joblessness in many countries, there will be a natural desire to keep government payrolls high, even at the risk of delaying efficiency improvements.

Leading from the front

Especially in a crisis, it's essential that government reformers lead from the front. Transformational-change efforts are short of leadership capacity, money, and management talent. Only leaders can ensure that among the myriad demands the economic crisis has spawned, government reform gets its due.

Why government reform is hard

Alastair Levy

Despite good intentions, many government reform programs are too slow, take too long, and achieve too little. Some of the barriers to success result from the inherent differences between the public and private sectors. Government's sheer scale and the need to integrate reform across several tiers of agencies and departments, for example, create a unique level of complexity. Effective decision making is complicated by the need to balance political and managerial priorities and to operate under the gaze of the public, the legislature, and the media.

Other barriers, arguably more of the public sector's own making, could be ameliorated if successful reform leaders focused on them by building capabilities and challenging inherited ways of working. There are five such barriers.

Alastair Levy is a consultant in McKinsey's London office.

1. The slow pace of reform often results directly from an ineffective approach to change management. The leadership may not be sufficiently urgent and intense. Frequently, the objectives of reform and accountability for making it happen are unclear, and the management of reform programs is weak. What's more, governments tend to ignore the possibility of building momentum through early wins and lack a developed performance culture. McKinsey's private-sector experience shows the importance of these dimensions of change.

2. Reform programs often lack the stretching, sustained ambition that transformational change requires. Typically, governments must raise their efficiency and effectiveness by 15 to 20 percent rather than the 2 to 3 percent they often aim for. Organizations can achieve a real break from the past only by challenging existing parameters—structure, size, capabilities, or processes.

Equally, only leaders can inspire the public sector's workforce to undertake difficult, sometimes painful reforms. These employees are typically motivated much less by financial incentives than by a sense of mission and peer pressure. To create the required momentum and support for change, government leaders must relentlessly engage with agency managers, civil servants, frontline staff, and professionals. And that's not all—the leaders must also educate consumers of public-sector services and the citizen body as a whole about the need for reform and for tough decisions on priorities. A well-informed public that demands better services will create pressure for change.

Not least important, change will happen only if government leaders develop and communicate reform strategies that identify the public sector's shape in ten or more years and show how to get there. These strategies will have to reflect trade-offs between what must be done to address urgent short-term needs, on the one hand, and to lay the foundations for a long-term transformation, on the other. A sustained drive to bring about rapid, tangible change must then follow.

Embedding successful reform

All too often, public- and private-sector reform programs alike make early progress but lose their initial energy and sense of purpose—

---

3. Public-sector leaders often lack the strong centers that their most successful business counterparts use to drive change through the organization. The scale of government and the legal separation of powers (for instance, among national, state, and local governments) mean that centrally controlled approaches to change can go only so far. This complexity, though, increases the need for sophisticated functions at the center of government and of major departments in order to set strategic priorities, allocate resources, manage performance, assess risk, and instill momentum for change across departments and agencies.

4. Governments are often awash with data but ill-equipped to use them in decision making. That makes it much harder for reform leaders to exercise the core functions of making and communicating effective decisions, whether about alternative models of service delivery or the allocation of scarce financial or human resources. The results of these shortcomings often include misspent resources, the loss of valuable time, and an inability to justify proposed reforms.

5. Not enough is done to engage public-sector employees. Transformational change requires a sustained and systematic effort to solicit the support, harness the expertise, and stimulate the creativity of the frontline administrative staff and of professionals such as doctors, nurses, teachers, and police officers. Government leaders—political or executive—can't delegate this responsibility or allow it to become diluted as change gets under way.

Two additional sidebars, "Public-sector reform in the United Kingdom" and "Undertaking reform in France," are available on mckinseyquarterly.com.

commonly when external conditions change. To make reforms endure, it will be necessary to weave them into the warp and weft of government.

Political leaders alone can't provide the intense focus and unyielding persistence required to drive a reform program. They typically need help from the kind of small, high-caliber team that business leaders appoint to steer key initiatives. Both France and the United Kingdom, for example, have relied heavily on high-quality "delivery units," which can be indispensable in propelling large-scale, far-reaching, and enduring transformations.

What's more, the momentum of change is more likely to be sustained if it's reinforced in tangible ways—in meaningful commitments to the public and the public-sector workforce and by the hard-wiring of reform objectives into budgets. Clear quantitative performance metrics and milestones are important too, so several governments (including those of New Zealand, the United Kingdom, and the US state of Virginia) have developed and applied detailed ones, which have helped them assess and communicate their progress in areas such as reducing crime and hospital waiting times and improving educational test scores.

Related articles on mckinseyquarterly.com
Boosting government productivity
Government as a business
Applying lean production to the public sector

Such actions at the center aren't enough, however. Government's scale and complexity make it essential to encourage departments and agencies to assume ownership of the reform effort. It will therefore be necessary to invest in developing change agents—leaders who act as role models for new and better ways to work—and to place them in key government units so that reforms reflecting the public's needs come down to the front line.

Finally, pilot projects provide a "proof of concept" and enable pioneers to demonstrate the possibilities of reform. If these efforts succeed—especially if they make an early impression on the public—they establish the case for broader, deeper reform.

• • •

Undertaking comprehensive, deep government reforms at a time of national and international crisis may seem daunting—perhaps even a distraction from the essential tasks of restoring sound finances and long-term prosperity. In fact, however, a purposeful, concerted, and determined transformation of government is essential for both of those purposes as well.

The authors wish to acknowledge the contributions of Alastair Levy, Allison Phillips, and David Skilling to this article.

Copyright © 2009 McKinsey & Company. All rights reserved.

We welcome your comments on this article. Please send them to quarterly_comments@mckinsey.com.

Reforming the public sector in a crisis:

An interview with Sweden's former prime minister

> Göran Persson has lived a story that should encourage leaders around the world: how to stay in power while pursuing a harsh crisis program that requires sacrifices throughout society.

Alastair Levy and Nick Lovegrove

Government leaders around the world face a daunting dual challenge: they must control and, in the long term, slash major budget deficits fueled by the economic crisis while at the same time improving the performance of the public sector so that it can meet its complex and ever-rising obligations.

Former Swedish prime minister Göran Persson is no stranger to that challenge. Even his political foes recognize his achievement.

In the early 1990s, Sweden suffered its deepest recession since the Great Depression. Although the Swedish crisis was homegrown, its causes and effects resemble the events unfolding in the world today. After years of strong domestic growth driven by easy credit and high leverage, a real-estate bubble burst, leading to the collapse and partial nationalization of the banking sector. Domestic demand plunged as the household savings ratio soared by 13 percentage points. In three years, public debt doubled, unemployment tripled, and the government budget deficit increased tenfold, to more than 10 percent of GDP, the largest in any OECD[1] country at the time.

Alastair Levy is a consultant in McKinsey's London office, and **Nick Lovegrove** is a director in the Washington, DC, office.

[1] Organisation for Economic Co-operation and Development.

Persson was appointed finance minister when the Social Democrats returned to power, after the 1994 elections, and became prime minister two years later. In order to regain the confidence of international lenders—and so pave the way for stability and sustainable growth—he knew that Sweden had to reduce its budget deficit dramatically. It took four years for the Swedish government to balance its budget. By 2006, when Persson and his party lost power in the general elections, the country had almost halved its public debt, to just above 40 percent of GDP.

Göran Persson recently spoke with McKinsey's Alastair Levy and Nick Lovegrove about what it takes to put troubled state finances in order and, at the same time, to improve the way the public sector works.

The *Quarterly*: *What is the prerequisite for implementing a successful crisis program?*

Göran Persson: The electorate must understand that drastic measures are required. A crisis program will hurt, and you will need a mandate from the voters if you are to succeed. This makes it difficult for an administration that is in power without such a mandate to take the lead. But it is a fantastic chance for the opposition, provided that there is broad awareness of the gravity of the situation. My party was elected in 1994 because we promised to carry out the harshest program with the deepest budget cuts and the sharpest tax increases.

The *Quarterly*: *What advice would you give incumbent leaders who don't have a mandate from the voters for instituting radical reform?*

Göran Persson

Vital statistics
Born January 20, 1949, in Vingåker, Sweden

Education
Studied social science at Örebro University, Sweden

Awarded honorary doctorates in medicine from Örebro University, Sweden (2004); in political science from Dankook University, South Korea (2004); and in political science from Tbilisi State University, Georgia (2006)

Career highlights
• Prime minister (1996–2006)

• Finance minister (1994–96)

• Minister of schools, Ministry of Education (1989–91)

• Municipal commissioner of Katrineholm (1984–89)

• Member of parliament (1979–84 and 1991–2007)

Fast facts
Serves as chairman of the board for Sveaskog, Sweden's largest forest owner

Is a part-time consultant and lecturer

Runs a small cattle and wood farm in Sörmland County, Sweden

Göran Persson: You have to make it absolutely clear that you are putting your office at stake; that you are prepared to call new elections or, if your parliamentary group is not behind you, to resign. The forces working against a harsh crisis program are very strong—almost every area of the public sector has its own vested interests—so any sign that you might waver in your commitment will doom the program to fail.

The Quarterly: *Please summarize the lessons you have learned about leading, designing, and implementing the process for putting state finances in order.*

Göran Persson: First, it is extremely important to be in the driver's seat. You must make it clear that you are responsible for the process and that you are prepared to put your position at stake. Second, the consolidation program must be designed so that the burdens are shared fairly. Public-sector cuts will hurt the most vulnerable people in society, so those who are better off need to contribute—for example, by paying higher taxes. Public support for tough policies would quickly deteriorate if they were not perceived as fair, and parliament would lose the political will to make hard decisions. Third, the consolidation program has to be designed as a comprehensive package; if you are in as deep trouble as we were, an ad hoc hodgepodge of measures will only have a limited chance of success. Moreover, by presenting the measures together, it becomes clear to all interest groups that they are not the only ones being asked to make sacrifices. It also has to be a front-loaded program. By starting with the most difficult measures, you demonstrate your resolve and increase the chances of achieving the early results, which will be important for getting the continued support that is critical for sustaining the effort.

Transparency is the fourth lesson. You must never play down the effects of the program's measures. On the contrary, remind the public again and again that this will hurt. It is one thing to get support in parliament for the program; it's another to stay in control during the implementation phase, when the measures become real for ordinary people in their daily lives. You must also be completely honest when you communicate with financial markets. Clarify assumptions and calculations. Don't use any bookkeeping tricks. Only then can you recover credibility; only then can the program earn legitimacy. Indeed, you should always go for conservative estimates. If, for instance, you estimate that economic growth will be 1.5 percent and you end up with 2.5 percent, you will have solved much of the credibility problem.

The Quarterly: *The electorate's patience is never endless. How much time do you have until it runs out?*

Göran Persson: You have two years. If you are not in command of the process by then, you will lose momentum and soon face the next election—where you will be replaced. We survived the 1998 election and were rewarded politically for what we had done by being reelected once more in 2002, when the good times returned and we were in firm control of the public finances.

The Quarterly: *Cutting the state budget during a crisis puts pressure on the public sector at a time when its services are perhaps more important than ever. How did you handle this problem?*

Göran Persson: Restoring the health of our public finances was the prerequisite for preserving the Swedish public sector in the long term, and this would not have been possible without sacrifices. One-third of our program consisted of tax increases, and two-thirds of spending cuts, both in the operational budgets of the central and local authorities and in the legislated levels of welfare transfers. We cut pensions, sick-leave compensation, and unemployment benefits, which hurt people who already had only small margins in their household finances. That shouldn't have been necessary in an ideal world, because lower welfare transfers reduced domestic demand and tax revenues and thus had a negative impact on growth and employment and a small net effect on the budget. But we had no choice. High interest rates made it necessary to regain the confidence of investors all over the world whose perception was that Sweden's generous welfare model was to blame for the crisis. In fact, it wasn't until we cut unemployment benefits and got into open conflict with the trade unions that market interest rates started coming down.

The Quarterly: *It's often said that with a crisis comes an opportunity for reform. Did you use this opportunity to improve the long-term performance of the public sector?*

Göran Persson: Yes, the cuts in government consumption became a driver of improved efficiency, since public authorities were forced to do the same job on unchanged or reduced budgets.

In addition, we pursued targeted policies with various objectives. One strategy—aiming to improve productivity, service quality, and freedom of choice—involved the liberalization of telecommunications, mail, railways, and other infrastructure industries. It also involved allowing privately run providers to compete with public ones in providing tax-financed services for the school system, health care, child care, and care for the elderly.

Another measure was to introduce information technology to broad layers of the population through a tax-deduction scheme that allowed workers to obtain a home computer under a favorable leasing agreement with their employers. The penetration of IT in Sweden during these years outpaced every other country in the world, which made it possible for authorities like the Tax Agency to go online at an early stage. Indeed, I'm quite confident today that information technology improves government productivity as well as the delivery of its services. More and more of the communication between Swedish public agencies and citizens now takes place on the Web, and many Swedes do their annual tax submissions over the Internet, allowing for a very efficient processing of taxes. I think our tax agency is one of the most efficient in the world and very much so because we are using modern technologies. We have one of the world's largest public sectors and, along with the Danes, the world's highest taxes, claiming almost 50 percent of GDP. We are also very good at collecting these taxes.

A third strategy was to give people with basic schooling the chance to complete a secondary education that would qualify them for university studies.[2] It was a straightforward system: an employed worker would get the equivalent of the unemployment benefit if he or she entered an adult-education program and if the employer agreed to replace him or her with an unemployed person. The employer's cost was unchanged, and the state's cost was limited to the education itself. Believe it or not, more than 10 percent of the workforce seized this opportunity between 1997 and 2002. It was mainly women who did so, and many went on to study at a university. When the business cycle turned up again, they became a very good resource on the labor market, not least in the public sector. This education scheme served a dual purpose: it eased the pain of unemployment and increased Sweden's long-term competitiveness by lifting the average competence level of the workforce.

The Quarterly: *What approach did you take to set efficiency targets and drive savings across the government?*

Göran Persson: We introduced three-year ceilings on public expenditure for each ministry. Within this ceiling, we gave the ministries and public agencies some flexibility to distribute their expenditure levels between the years in each three-year frame as long as they reached their final target. These caps on expenditure were the main driving force. Sweden has a decentralized system of government, so even though we set the guidelines it was up to each authority to figure out how to fulfill its service obligations while still achieving the required spending cuts. The budget cuts for the authorities and agencies amounted to a grand total of 11 percent from 1995 to 1998. After that, we built in an efficiency factor based on productivity in the private-service sector, which the public agencies had to match. By doing so, we continued to put pressure on them to improve their efficiency and produce more or the same for less. The result was that they started to examine expenditures that they had regarded as

---

[2] The *Kunskapslyftet*, or "Knowledge Lift," a Swedish adult-education program.

impossible to influence—for instance the location and rental cost of their offices—and they also became more careful about whom to employ and about developing the staff they already had.

The Quarterly: *As the political leader, what was your experience with trying to get the civil servants on board and making them partners in the initiative?*

Göran Persson: They had never experienced a crisis of this magnitude. Some reacted to it as a professional opportunity to perform a very significant task. Others felt betrayed by the cuts and that it was not their role to deal with productivity or efficiency issues. In the end, though, it was quite easy to get the civil servants on board because they were all conscious of the crisis and its dangers.

The Quarterly: *Did you make many personnel changes, particularly in important positions?*

Göran Persson: Only gradually and in a small way. It's very easy to get rid of people, but it's difficult to find new ones that you can be sure

Exhibit

Sweden's budget and reforms under Persson

Government net borrowing/net lending as % of GDP

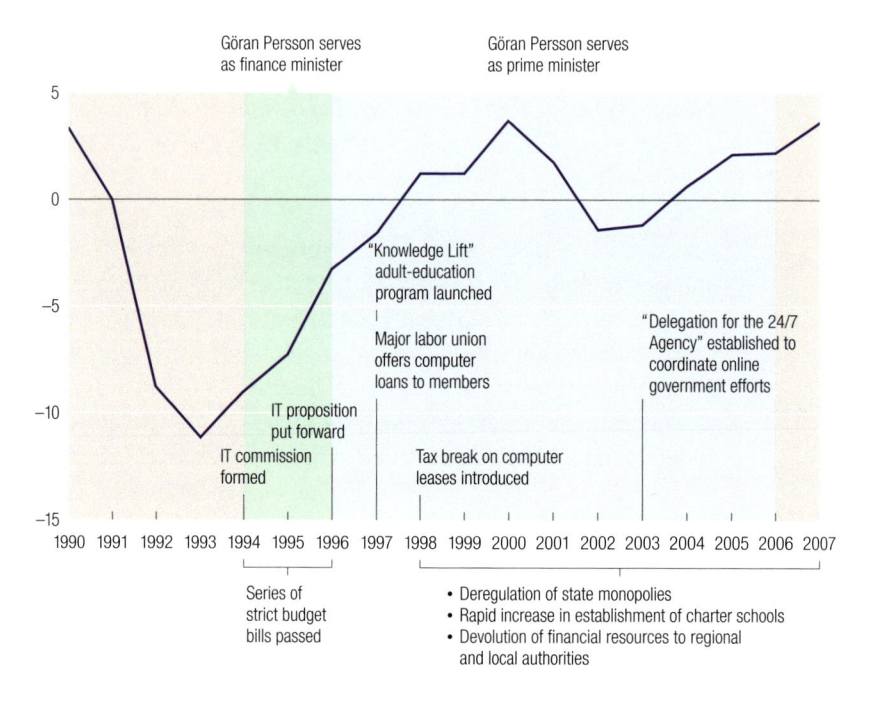

Göran Persson serves as finance minister

Göran Persson serves as prime minister

"Knowledge Lift" adult-education program launched

Major labor union offers computer loans to members

"Delegation for the 24/7 Agency" established to coordinate online government efforts

IT proposition put forward

IT commission formed

Tax break on computer leases introduced

Series of strict budget bills passed

- Deregulation of state monopolies
- Rapid increase in establishment of charter schools
- Devolution of financial resources to regional and local authorities

Source: *OECD Factbook 2009: Economic, Environmental and Social Statistics*, Organisation for Economic Co-operation and Development (OECD); McKinsey analysis

are better. So I find that it's often wiser to stick with the staff you have. It is, after all, the politicians who are responsible for restoring order in the country's finances, so it's up to them to lead, support, educate, and stimulate those who carry it out. Sometimes you are successful in this regard; sometimes you fail.

The Quarterly: *Did you set up some kind of machinery at the center of government to monitor departments and agencies and to intervene, when necessary, to move things along?*

Göran Persson: No, we did not. We were in such acute crisis that we had to move as quickly as we could, so we executed the program without reflecting in detail on its implementation. We monitored two indicators very closely; one was the bottom line of the state finances and the other Sweden's interest rate levels, because financial markets reacted very quickly to the program and its progress. If I had to do it all again, I would perhaps set up some centralized unit just to monitor progress and to spread ideas and best practices.

The Quarterly: *Did the process lead to significant changes in the way government worked and the way it developed and delivered its services?*

Göran Persson: The efficiency targets had positive consequences for public services, at both the state and local levels. At the local level, the targets encouraged public agencies to collaborate, leading to better services for the people. Similarly, as a response to the remit we gave government agencies—such as the tax and social-security authorities—to improve their efficiency to private-sector levels, they started talking to each other and cooperating more closely than before. We didn't plan these changes, but they were positive nevertheless.

The cabinet was another example of change. People tend to view it as a tight-knit team, but it is not. Ministers are constantly competing with each other for the available resources. This was not the case during the crisis. In fact, it was the only time in my 15 years as a cabinet member when I felt that I was leading a real team where everybody was prepared to contribute and to help each other. Why? Because we all understood that the budget deficit, if left unchecked, could destroy the public sector as we knew it. We also knew that beating the crisis required us to work as a team, because if just one minister leaks to the media that his or her area of responsibility is carrying an unfair share of the burden, the whole process will soon break down. You must realize that the cabinet is one thing; the parliament, however, is something else, and you can never take the support of your parliamentary group for granted. If there is the slightest dissension between your ministers, their support groups in parliament could block bills that you are bringing to the assembly. This would be very serious. A budget-consolidation process of this kind requires not only a state budget: the budget needs to be followed by perhaps 50 or 100 different initiatives that all have to pass through parliament. So if you cannot keep your team together, you will find yourself on a very slippery slope.

Related articles on mckinseyquarterly.com
Sweden's growth paradox
Perspectives on change: A former chief of staff reflects
Public-private partnerships as a development engine

The Quarterly: *What levers did you have at the center for influencing change at ministries that were not making good on their efficiency targets?*

Göran Persson: Each ministry had its own bottom-line target, and if it didn't make good on that target there would be a discussion with the ministries' top managers. Where needed, I or my finance minister became directly involved in discussions with departmental ministers. In doing so, we suggested ways to move forward, but we would never tell them what to do. Giving direct and detailed orders would have broken the internal ethics of the budget-consolidation process—which we had agreed to achieve as a team. It would also have given the finance minister or prime minister ownership of somebody else's task.

In fact, what is taught in the private sector about the importance of building well-functioning top teams applies to government as well, except that it's harder in government. Much more transparency is required, and every little detail can become public knowledge. Moreover, your ownership of the process is under constant threat from the opposition and, perhaps, your own parliamentary group. This makes it essential to build loyalty and solidarity within your team of ministers or else you won't achieve anything. Political leadership is often said to be about visions and ideas. But it is also about ensuring that a transparent public organization can achieve productive results in its daily work not only once but again and again every year, and under constant external pressure.

Copyright © 2009 McKinsey & Company. All rights reserved.

We welcome your comments on this article. Please send them to quarterly_comments@mckinsey.com.

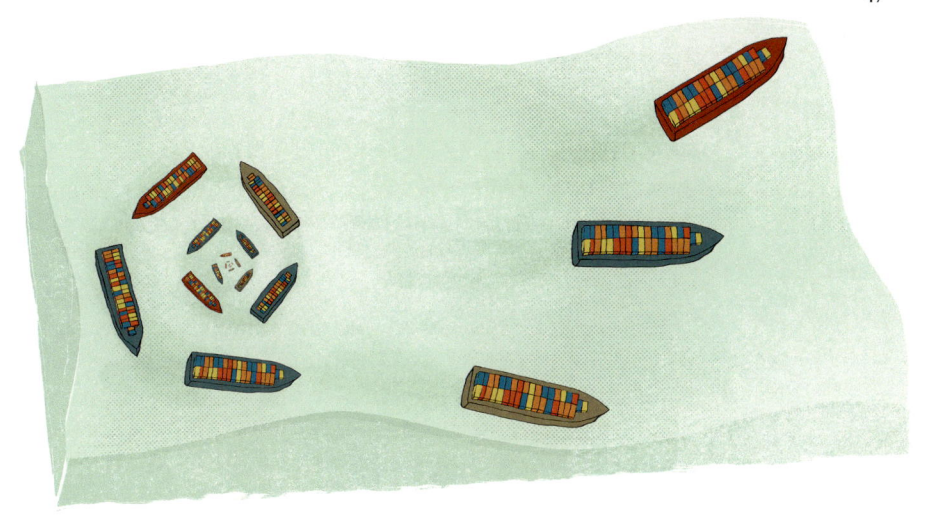

New challenges for Asia's governments

As the roles of the region's governments expand and change, they must transform their capacity and performance.

David Skilling

David Skilling is an associate principal in McKinsey's Singapore office.

Across the world, the role of government in the economy is expanding as a result of the implosion of credit markets and the subsequent sharp decline in economic activity, as well as concerns about social and political stability.

In the West, this expansion has provoked a debate about whether it's just a temporary response to great economic and financial turbulence or if it represents a discontinuity that will redefine government's economic role in a significant and enduring way.

But in much of Asia, the intensity of the West's debate on the role of government is hard to fathom. Big government hasn't returned to Asia; it never left. Long before the current crisis, governments in fast-growing Asian economies such as Malaysia and Singapore routinely endeavored to shape economic outcomes by developing and implementing industrial policy, managing exchange rates, deploying reserves, and using state-owned assets. China's blend of Marx and markets—Deng Xiaoping's "capitalism with Chinese characteristics"—never envisioned a withering away of the state.

So for many who live or do business in this dynamic region, ideological angst about government's role in the economy misses the point. In Asia, political and business leaders are far more apt to focus on what works.

This pragmatism will be vital over the coming years. Clearly, the crisis will require significant change. Asia is less exposed to financial turmoil than the West is, because Asian countries responded to the previous decade's regional crisis by improving their current-account positions, accumulating reserves, and ensuring that their banking systems operated prudently. But the crisis has exposed the limits of the region's dominant economic-growth model. Asian economies will need alternative sources of growth to compensate for the rapid fall in demand from Western markets. The export-led model that propelled many Asian economies so effectively for the past 30 years must be adapted to a different global economic context.

The crisis, and its longer-term implications, will also pose challenges to the way Asia's governments operate, requiring continued adjustments to their roles. In particular, Asian governments are likely to become more prominent in three areas over the coming years.

Government as principal investor. Many Asian governments already have significant holdings of financial and physical assets, controlled by commercially oriented state-owned enterprises, sovereign-wealth funds, and the like. These government holdings will probably expand further as a result of the ongoing accumulation of reserves and the organic growth of existing publicly held assets. This expansion will raise difficult strategic questions about the best way to use a government's balance sheet. Will the goal be to maximize returns on assets, or will governments use them to pursue other development objectives—for example, by applying reserves to domestic infrastructure projects rather than foreign investments? To the extent that governments increasingly use their balance sheets to boost economic growth, careful thought will be required to preserve the efficiency and returns of assets.

Government as alliance builder. As prospects for another round of multilateral tariff reductions

Read more about the public sector and business on mckinseyquarterly.com.

Public-sector companies can match the performance of their private-sector counterparts and even become world-class players. Read **"Improving performance at state-owned enterprises."**

In the wake of the global recession, governments around the world are spending billions to stimulate growth and bail out vulnerable domestic industries and companies. Political-risk consultant Ian Bremmer discusses the implications in **"State capitalism and the crisis."**

falter and protectionist pressures rise around the world, Asian countries will find the possibility of regional economic collaboration more appealing. Many of them are too small to achieve minimum efficient economic scale. Fortunately, they have ample opportunity to expand regional free trade, enhance regulatory efficiency, and deepen capital pools through arrangements such as joint currency areas, regional investment funds, and regional bond or equity exchanges. Borders and national sovereignty will remain, of course, and an EU-style arrangement has no real likelihood of emerging in the region, but Asian governments will probably start to think harder about which functions they should handle independently and which would be more efficient if shared.

Related articles on mckinseyquarterly.com
Organizing for effectiveness in the public sector
Reassessing China's state-owned enterprises
Spurring performance in China's state-owned enterprises

Government as economic strategist. Asian governments have long shown a willingness to shape and develop their economies deliberately rather than limit themselves to providing a stable platform for private competition. As the global economy's competitive intensity increases, these governments will probably remain actively involved in attracting capital and labor and in developing skills to bolster competitiveness. Governments across Asia are also likely to use stimulus packages and longer-term measures to help their economies make the transition to a more regionally oriented growth model.

• • •

In Asia as elsewhere, the role of government is changing and expanding. Not all of the innovations will succeed, but governments in the region may pioneer new approaches—to regional economic integration, economic strategy, and the management of government balance sheets—that may hold lessons for the rest of the world. To handle these new responsibilities, governments must urgently transform their ability to perform. They need much greater access to the people and expertise some new functions will require. They'll have to develop new organizational structures facilitating far more effective collaboration among government agencies, across countries, and between the public and private sectors. And they must create new operating models that enable government agencies to respond much more rapidly and responsively to external events. Business as usual won't be sufficient. o

Copyright © 2009 McKinsey & Company. All rights reserved.

We welcome your comments on this article. Please send them to quarterly_comments@mckinsey.com.

Special report
Inside the US stimulus program

53
Energy:
Investing in efficiency

56
Health care:
Taking medical records online

59
Broadband:
Improving access

Introduction:
Implications for three industries

The US government is beginning to spend vast sums to jump-start the economy. The opportunities for the private sector are huge, but so are the changes it must make to benefit from them.

Joshua Crossman, Fred Kneip, and Jon Wilkins

Josh Crossman is an associate principal in McKinsey's Seattle office; **Fred Kneip** is an associate principal in the Washington, DC, office, where **Jon Wilkins** is a principal.

The American Recovery and Reinvestment Act of 2009 (ARRA) represents the largest government intervention in the US economy since the New Deal. The total cost comes to a towering 5.4 percent of GDP—almost equal to federal expenditures on everything but military and mandated social programs during 2008. More than 70 percent of the money is to be spent by the end of fiscal year 2010.

A plan of such scale and reach comes with risks of mismanagement, perhaps even fraud, as funding flows to states and localities. But the act also portends vastly different terms of engagement between the government and the private sector. From energy to high tech to health care and beyond, major sectors of the US economy will feel the effects of policy, spending, and regulatory changes embodied in the stimulus and perhaps in a broader set of government interventions that are still under discussion.

The plans for the energy sector exemplify many aspects of the new approach (see "Energy: Investing in efficiency," in this report). The Obama administration has set three sweeping goals: to create millions of clean-energy jobs over the next decade, to cut oil imports by two million barrels a day over the same period, and to slash greenhouse gas emissions by 80 percent, to levels below those of 1990, by the year 2050. The ARRA's $97 billion[1] in energy-

---

[1] Of the $97 billion, $46 billion will be spent on energy-specific projects. An additional $21 billion represents energy-related tax credits. The final $30 billion consists of broader spending initiatives with an energy component (such as funds for building renovations that include energy-efficiency investments).

related funding is only the first step. Separate energy and climate bills now under debate include far-reaching provisions, such as cap-and-trade polices for carbon dioxide emissions. The 2010 budget would establish a regulatory framework to recast the energy sector's fundamental economics.

In high tech, government spending will touch nearly every subsector, with projects running the gamut from airport security installations and software for tracking student performance to systems integration work in federal agencies and optical fiber for new rural broadband networks (see "Broadband: Improving access," in this report). Our analysis shows that $60 billion will be targeted directly at high tech and telecommunications. Including indirect government technology outlays, the level of expenditure rises to well over $200 billion: every major construction project funded by the ARRA will need computers, software, and IT services, for example (exhibit).

As the new reality takes shape, companies in the affected industries must rethink their strategies and organization. Some may be skeptical of deep engagement with the government, while others will leap at the opportunities offered by the stimulus. For companies that want to participate, developing the capabilities needed to flourish in this new world should become a critical priority. Some companies that haven't dealt with the government before will need to develop new skills—in contracting, for instance.

The health care sector offers examples of how product development, pricing,

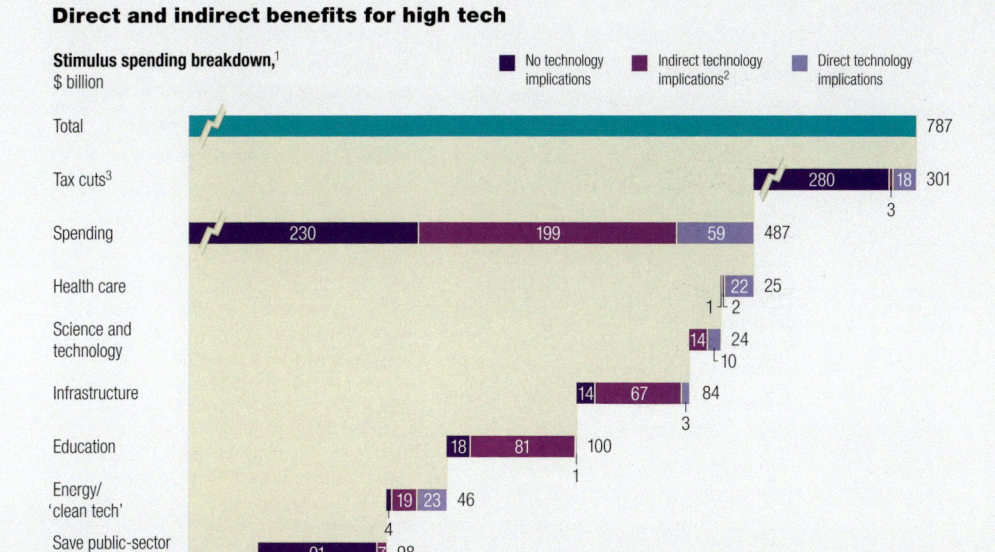

Exhibit

Direct and indirect benefits for high tech

Stimulus spending breakdown,[1]
$ billion

Legend: No technology implications | Indirect technology implications[2] | Direct technology implications

Category	No tech	Indirect tech	Direct tech	Total
Total				787
Tax cuts[3]	280		18 / 3	301
Spending	230	199	59	487
Health care		22	1 / 2	25
Science and technology		14	10	24
Infrastructure	14	67	3	84
Education	18	81	1	100
Energy/'clean tech'	19	23	4	46
Save public-sector jobs and services	91		7	98
Social aid	102		9	111

[1] Figures may not sum to totals, because of rounding.
[2] Refers to categories of expenditure that could result in technology spending. For example, spending on new bridge or road construction could generate technology-related spending on software (eg, computer-aided design) and traffic control technology.
[3] Refers to tax cuts for use of "clean technology"—ie, technology that employs renewable materials and energy sources.

Source: US Congressional Budget Office (2/13/2009); House Committee on Appropriations

and channel strategies could change. The government will spend $40 billion[2] to subsidize the use of electronic medical records (see "Health care: Taking medical records online," in this report). Technology vendors will thus have a chance to serve a new market: small and midsize physicians' offices, often with fewer than five MDs each. Government spending should increase the adoption of electronic records from 5 percent of doctors now to 90 percent by 2019, according to the Congressional Budget Office. Vendors in the e-health arena (hardware, software, and IT services companies) must therefore rethink marketing strategies that target only larger companies. Many must not only learn how to offer flexible, physician-friendly products (such as software-as-a-service[3] systems) but also reorient channel strategies to accommodate a sprawling, fragmented market of 400,000 doctors' offices.

An increased government presence in many sectors will also force companies to test new organizational structures that knit together disconnected parts of the enterprise. The product-development, sales, marketing, and government affairs functions, for example, will need better models of collaboration. Already, many companies are setting up "war rooms" that assemble cross-functional teams to identify, prioritize, and capture the opportunities the stimulus spending presents. These teams, combining sales representatives with managers who have regional, product, or public-sector expertise, focus initially on line-by-line analysis of the stimulus act and then identify strategies for entering the new markets. One technology company, for example, found $1 billion in revenue opportunities after embracing an organizational blueprint that stressed expanded partnerships with prime government contractors.

Companies will need to formalize these arrangements by weaving their public-sector and government affairs groups into the process of developing strategy and monitoring its execution. A leading private-equity fund learned some of these lessons quickly. Its first response to the new environment was to have its government affairs team work actively with regulators, but only on issues directly affecting the private-equity industry. The fund soon realized, however, that stimulus expenditures would have dramatic effects, beyond relatively narrow finance industry issues, on many companies in its portfolio. Now it's reorienting and bulking up its government affairs team. Similarly, the government relations unit of a health care company has joined forces with marketing and sales. Realigned incentives and responsibilities are keeping the unit's managers in close contact with both customers and regulators, so that the company can quickly learn how new regulations will affect product design.

In short, the public sector's terrain is expanding dramatically, and the private sector is responding. Companies that move with both speed and deliberation should be able to manage the risks of this transition and to find its opportunities. o

[2] We estimate that the ultimate net cost to the government is $25 billion, because the $40 billion in total spending should be offset by around $15 billion from cost savings enabled by the investment and penalties paid by nonparticipants.
[3] Internet-based systems that can be tailored to the requirements of physicians and eliminate the need for expensive specialized hardware and the associated cost of support.

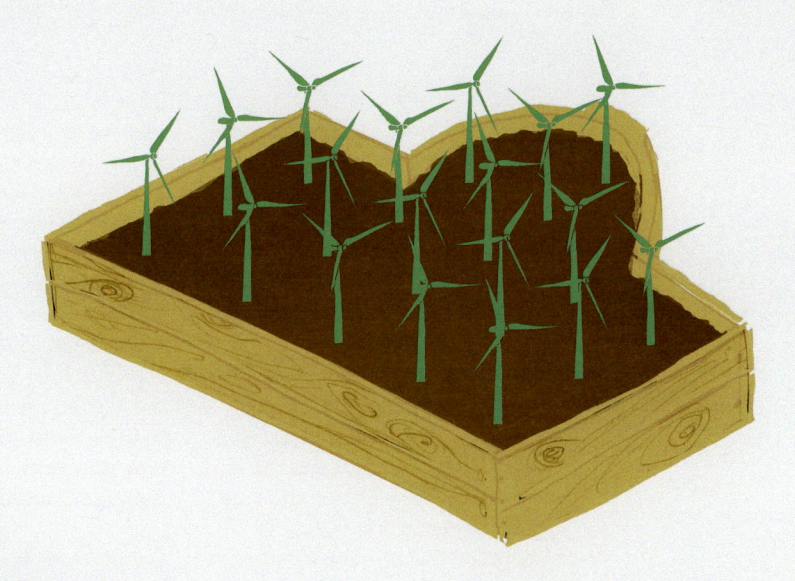

Energy:
Investing in efficiency

There may be tensions among the administration's goals, but nearly $100 billion in new spending on energy-related projects will have a huge impact.

Scott Jacobs and Rob McNish

Scott Jacobs is a consultant in McKinsey's San Francisco office, and Rob McNish is a director in the Washington, DC, office.

The American Recovery and Reinvestment Act (ARRA) provides nearly $100 billion in energy-related funding, much of it to boost the efficiency and reduce the environmental impact of US energy use (exhibit). The speed and scale of the government's commitment has the potential to dislocate strategies and disrupt market shares in the energy sector for years to come. With the government assuming the role of primary banker and customer in many energy markets, executives must decide whether to rethink, and in some cases completely redraw, their capital and marketing plans.

As industry executives wrestle with these decisions, the government itself must come to terms with a series of competing objectives embedded in the stimulus. The ARRA, for example, has a bias toward job creation and "shovel readiness," which could favor established over nascent renewable-energy players, potentially compromising the long-term goal of transforming the US energy base. The act also relies heavily on public–private coinvestment, which may be difficult to pull off given the growing concern among business leaders about entanglement with the public sector, not to mention the current state of credit markets. Finally, the ARRA emphasizes energy efficiency, a goal to be met primarily through the efforts of state and local governments that aren't fully prepared to deploy the proposed funds.

Three big numbers help paint a picture of the forces the ARRA will unleash and of the tensions inherent in it: 300,000 (the number of jobs the administration hopes it will create and retain), $100 billion (the level of private-sector coinvestment the administration hopes to unleash), and a 20-fold spending increase (on many forms of energy efficiency).

Jobs
The bias to near-term job creation means that more mature technologies will probably receive the majority of funds—dampening the ability of the stimulus to accelerate the learning curves that new technologies must progress down as they mature. Indeed, more established players and proven technologies may increase their competitive lead over smaller players with developing ones.

Such tensions are particularly evident in the solar subsector: larger companies will find it easier to tap into renewable-energy loan guarantees because these players can make a more credible case that they will add manufacturing capacity and create jobs. Furthermore, the investment tax credits in the stimulus can be used as grants for people who buy solar products—by definition, from companies with existing inventories and manufacturing capacity.

The government appears to recognize this potential "maturity bias," as the stimulus also contains substantial increases in funding for research and development. There's $400 million, for example, to finance a new Advanced Research Projects Agency-Energy (ARPA-E) modeled after the Defense Advanced Research Projects Agency (DARPA), which helped create the Internet, among many other innovations. Nearly $800 million of the money will be used to create energy-frontier research centers. Still, the general orientation toward short-term job creation is strong, and countervailing forces probably won't fully overcome the maturity bias.

One likely implication is an uptick in partnerships among players both big and small. Teaming up with other companies can help all of them enhance their contracting positions with the government and meet the insistence of federal agencies on rapid, integrated solutions. Alliances also can improve access to capital for smaller players, while boosting the odds that their new technologies will capture the attention of established government contractors.

Private-sector coinvestment
Nearly all of the federal funding initiatives require coinvestment by the private sector. The $6 billion Innovative Technology Loan Guarantee Program, for example, aims to support $60 billion in loans from private-sector banks for

Exhibit

Energy-related stimulus spending

American Recovery and Reinvestment Act stimulus spending on energy by category,[1] $ billion

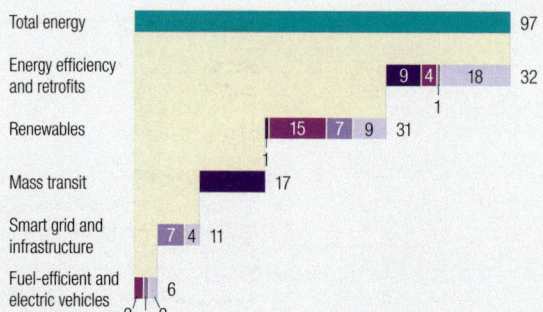

Category	Total	Breakdown
Total energy	97	
Energy efficiency and retrofits	32	9 / 4 / 1 / 18
Renewables	31	15 / 7 / 1 / 9
Mass transit	17	
Smart grid and infrastructure	11	7 / 4
Fuel-efficient and electric vehicles	6	2 / 1 / 2

- Spending outside Department of Energy (DOE)
- Tax incentives
- DOE loans
- DOE grants

[1] Figures may not sum to totals, because of rounding.

Source: US Congressional Budget Office (2/13/2009); House Committee on Appropriations

renewable-energy projects. Recipients of grants for smart grids and the manufacture of batteries must finance, from their own coffers, an amount equal to what they receive from the government.

That approach encourages responsible project proposals and the sharing of risk with the private sector but may slow or perhaps limit the deployment of federal funds. Companies incur transaction costs securing government money, and it remains to be seen how many of them will risk significant amounts of their own—often, in the millions of dollars—to craft solid proposals and have the government review their applications. In addition, energy players have long struggled with the inconsistency and uncertainty of US policy, exemplified by the annual renewal of production tax credits for renewables (specifically, wind power) and policy flip-flops on nuclear power. Anxiety about the potential ramifications of coinvesting or otherwise partnering with the government compounds the problem; energy players are watching with interest the fate of automotive and financial-services companies as their ties with the government deepen.

Despite the administration's clear policy direction, no short-term stimulus, nor even the longer-term energy policy bills now under development, will completely resolve the suspicions of private-sector investors. Yet competitive pressures could serve as an important motivator: the prospect that companies may secure government support could inspire their rivals to seek it as well.

Energy-efficiency spending

About one-third of the $97 billion in energy-related funds will be allocated to energy efficiency investments. The administration hopes that they will help overcome key market imperfections—such as information gaps and misaligned incentives—that now discourage businesses, consumers, and the public sector from undertaking many net-present-value-positive efficiency investments.[1] Big-ticket items include $4.5 billion for retrofits of federal buildings (20 times 2008 spending) and $5 billion for the Department of Energy's (DOE) weatherization program (another 20-fold increase over last year).

An obvious challenge: to deploy much of the efficiency funding, the DOE will rely on state and local administrative bodies that aren't fully prepared for such high budget increases. Another issue is whether or not, and when, companies in the energy efficiency supply chain can ramp up to meet spikes in demand for building materials and devices and for the skilled workers needed to use them in projects. A related question is whether the near-term spending surge will generate sustained investments or instead end up as a one-time jolt.

Policy makers and the public at large should be realistic about the ability of any short-term spending program, no matter how well conceived, to transform a large, complex sector in a fundamental way. Yet executives in the energy sector shouldn't underestimate the impact that $97 billion, quickly deployed, will have on its future shape. Despite the tensions inherent in the stimulus package, technology learning curves will probably accelerate, innovative new players should gain a measure of strength, and successful programs sustained by future government support are likely to emerge. The task before companies now is to develop careful, coherent plans for dealing with the government as a new shaping force in the energy sector.

[1] See, for example, Diana Farrell, Scott S. Nyquist, and Matthew C. Rogers, "Making the most of the world's energy resources," mckinseyquarterly.com, February 2007, and "Curbing the growth of global energy demand," mckinseyquarterly.com, July 2007; and Diana Farrell and Jaana K. Remes, "How the world should invest in energy efficiency," mckinseyquarterly.com, July 2008.

Health care:
Taking medical records online

EMR is a technology whose time has come. Whether or not it can deliver on its promise, it will change health care profoundly.

Sanjeev Agarwal, Brian Milch, and Steve Van Kuiken

Sanjeev Agarwal is a principal, **Brian Milch** is a consultant, and **Steve Van Kuiken** is a director in McKinsey's New Jersey office.

The Obama administration has committed an estimated $40 billion in funding for health care IT as part of the American Recovery and Reinvestment Act (ARRA). These funds are intended to accelerate the shift from today's silo-ridden and usually paper-based arrangements to a system that coordinates information more effectively and efficiently, with IT supporting a wide range of medical decisions.

The ARRA sets up incentives and penalties that will prompt health care providers to upgrade their IT systems rapidly to reach the act's standards for "meaningful use" of electronic medical records (EMR). Medical payers should be prime beneficiaries of the change, because health care costs may fall and treatments should become more effective and less error prone. And IT vendors will find that this fast-moving market demands new strategies. Left unanswered is the contentious issue of how the more aggressive use of EMR affects privacy. The substantial flow of dollars into EMR suggests that the administration feels confident that government and industry, working together, will resolve the problem.

Health care providers

The heart of the Obama package is raising EMR adoption rates among health care providers. Most surveys show that cost is the chief barrier, though the economics of adoption are already improving. Even without the stimulus, growing numbers of physicians and hospitals will probably switch to electronic records to drive down costs and improve the management of care. The stimulus package gives a significant boost to this effort (exhibit). First, it will provide incentive payments totaling $36.5 billion for hospitals and physicians' groups, requiring them to show that they are making meaningful use of the technology, starting in 2011. Second, it will extract escalating penalties, charged against Medicare and Medicaid payments, from providers that haven't met this standard by 2015.

For private-practice physicians, the incentives and penalties are a powerful prod. Over five years, Medicare incentives will amount to as much as $44,000 per doctor, probably more than enough to cover the cost of installing EMR, particularly as systems using software-as-a-service (SaaS) technology[1] go mainstream. The Congressional Budget Office estimates that adoption rates will climb to 90 percent by 2019.

For larger in-patient providers, principally hospitals, the new regime requires bigger and more complex IT systems and therefore higher long-haul costs to manage and maintain them. The stimulus grants won't cover much of this sprawling investment, so to get the full benefit the big health care providers must ensure that their physicians make complete use of EMR. They'll also need to retool their workflows to take advantage of the switch from a paper-based system to an automated one. Some providers may decide that EMR isn't worthwhile—payments and penalties notwithstanding.

Health insurers

Payers stand to gain the most from greater reliance on IT. Better information promises to cut costs and improve medical care's overall quality and efficiency. But to succeed, payers will need closer, more trusting relationships with hospitals and doctors to support implementation of clinical-decision-support (CDS) systems that ferry, organize, and analyze information from medical records and help clinicians choose the best course of treatment by weighing statistical evidence on the efficacy of various types of care and balancing them against their costs and insurance coverage limits.

Payers should gain greater influence over physicians by ensuring that the CDS systems they use have accurate medical information (and patient-specific cost information), which will help them improve their clinical performance. These companies must scrupulously ensure that this information is unbiased, however, because physicians will discount recommendations that strike

[1] Internet-based systems that can be tailored to the requirements of physicians and eliminate the need for expensive specialized hardware and the associated cost of support.

Exhibit

Stimulating adoption of electronic medical records

Adoption of electronic medical records clinical software, %

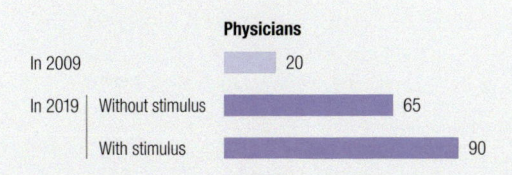

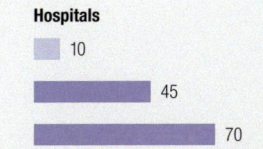

		Physicians	Hospitals
In 2009		20	10
In 2019	Without stimulus	65	45
	With stimulus	90	70

Source: US Congressional Budget Office; McKinsey analysis

them as unduly influenced by cost-reduction imperatives. As records systems spread through the medical community, they will create large pools of longitudinal patient data. Payers will tap this information to deepen their knowledge of effective treatments. Ultimately, the information will help payers make better decisions on reimbursement for diagnostics, pharmaceuticals, and medical devices.

IT vendors
Over the next decade, we estimate, hospitals and physicians will lay out approximately $170 billion on EMR. Hospitals will be responsible for the lion's share, 75 percent—more than ten times what they get in incentive payments. The spending will fall in three areas: hardware (roughly 40 percent), software (around 30 percent), and services (another 30 percent). To tap these opportunities, IT vendors as a group must rethink their strategies by identifying the software and services that the new IT-enabled world requires and upgrading their product portfolios to meet the meaningful-use standard. Partnerships among hardware, systems, and clinical-software vendors will improve their return on investment and play a critical role in clarifying the new environment and the demands of the health care providers.

Although seemingly a small portion of spending on health care, the ARRA's medical IT provisions could represent a turning point in the whole sector's evolution. Some players will benefit and others suffer, but all will be affected and may need to adjust their strategies. O

• • •

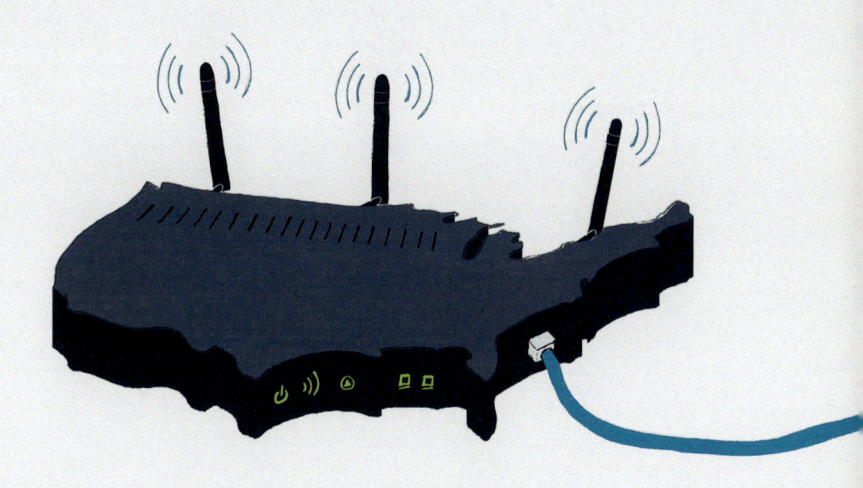

Broadband:
Improving access

The United States is behind many rich and even not-so-rich countries in broadband Internet access. The Obama administration aims to expand it.

Joshua Crossman, Dilip Wagle, and Jon Wilkins

Joshua Crossman is an associate principal in McKinsey's Seattle office, where **Dilip Wagle** is a principal; **Jon Wilkins** is a principal in the Washington, DC, office.

The United States ranks an unflattering 15th in global broadband penetration. The American Recovery and Reinvestment Act (ARRA) will sink $7.2 billion into improving the US broadband infrastructure. In parallel, the Federal Communications Commission is defining a national strategy to set formal US broadband targets. The stimulus plan's near-term goal, however, is clear: improving access among unserved and underserved US communities.

This spending could have complex and powerful effects on the companies that broadband technology touches. It represents a significant part of projected telecom capital spending over the next few years (exhibit)—up to 50 percent if the downturn continues to inhibit private-sector spending. The choice of wireline rather than wireless technologies as the preferred delivery vehicle, for example, will have major competitive implications for service providers. The impact will likely spill over to consumer electronics, because wireless access favors handhelds and smart phones, while wireline drives demand for PCs.

Let's consider a few examples of the strategic complexity ahead.

Large incumbent telephone companies
In an effort to avoid the regulations and oversight that the stimulus funding will bring, most large telco incumbents probably won't apply. They may instead seek indirect benefits—for example, by encouraging applications for grants by public institutions such as community colleges, which they would support as service providers. Still unresolved is what happens when an incumbent telco's competitors, such as cable

Exhibit

Investing in broadband

Recent and projected US broadband access spending, $ billion

Scenario 1: Projected investment growth in broadband[1]

(Chart showing values from 2006–2012, 0–7 $ billion, with layers: Fiber, DSL, Cable, Wireless, Federal stimulus investment; 44% labeled)

Scenario 2: Flat investment growth in broadband

(Chart showing values from 2006–2012, 0–7 $ billion, with layers: Fiber, DSL, Cable, Wireless, Federal stimulus investment; 51% labeled)

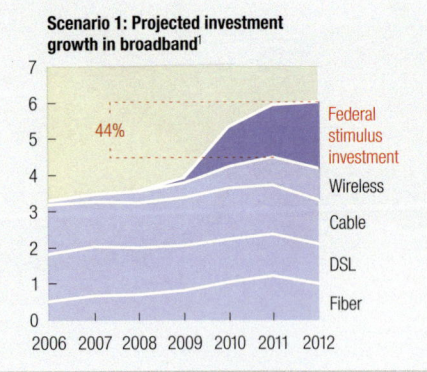

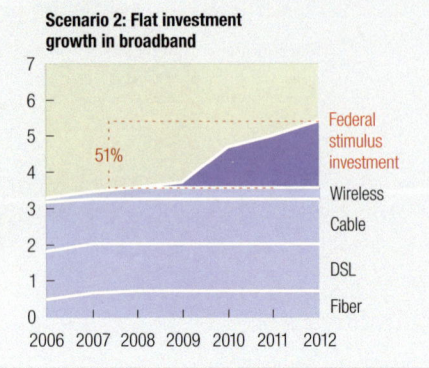

Federal funding will:
- Subsidize up to 80% of projects that would not be feasible without stimulus investment
- Focus on unserved and underserved areas through National Telecommunications and Information Administration and rural areas through Department of Agriculture
- Support a national broadband plan, but will be granted before plan is finalized
- Be spread across all 50 states
- Prioritize open infrastructure and partnerships among many Internet service providers (ISPs)

[1] Projection from Gartner Dataquest.

Source: American Recovery and Reinvestment Act (ARRA); Gartner Dataquest Market Statistics 2008; US Congressional Budget Office; US Congressional Record

and wireless companies, apply for funding in a region underserved by the incumbent, potentially damaging its economic position.

Large wireless players

Other forces could be at work among large wireless providers, which are eager to roll out next-generation broadband networks in broader commercial markets. To aid those efforts, some wireless companies may seek subsidies to build public-safety networks using new broadband technology, which the ARRA explicitly aims to promote. Because the technology for these networks is also the foundation for new fourth-generation (4G) commercial wireless networks, companies that receive funding would in effect be getting an R&D subsidy that may give them an edge in the 4G race.

Rural providers

For regulators, the challenge here will be developing an effective metric to gauge the policy's overall impact and social returns. Would it be better, for instance, to give rural providers grants so that they could offer access to a few customers who now have no broadband service or to use the available funds to improve broadband speeds? Some competitive crosscurrents must also be addressed: for example, will the act finance rural telcos when cable operators already provide broadband services to the same areas?

Copyright © 2009 McKinsey & Company. All rights reserved.

We welcome your comments on this article. Please send them to quarterly_comments@mckinsey.com.

The full versions of the articles in this report are available on mckinseyquarterly.com.

Weighing the US government's response to the crisis:
A dialogue

Two business strategists, Lowell Bryan and Richard Rumelt, discuss the prospects for the economy, companies, and workers.

Allen P. Webb

Eight months have passed since the collapse of Lehman Brothers punctuated the global financial crisis, touching off reverberations in the real economy that continue to reshape the business environment. In the depths of the crisis, the *Quarterly* asked Lowell Bryan, a director in McKinsey's New York office, and Richard Rumelt, a professor of strategy at UCLA's Anderson School of Management, to weigh in on the situation. Bryan's "Leading through uncertainty" and Rumelt's "Strategy in a structural break" appeared in *McKinsey Quarterly*, 2009 Number 1.

In late April, McKinsey's Allen Webb went back to Bryan and Rumelt and asked them to reflect on the government's response to the crisis. Edited excerpts of their conversation follow.

The *Quarterly*: *What do you think of the US policy response to the financial crisis?*

Lowell Bryan: I sit and marvel at it. It was very hard for me to get used to the idea that the federal government—and I'm talking not just about the Federal Reserve but the Treasury—would be as quick to

Allen Webb is a member of the *McKinsey Quarterly*'s board of editors.

Lowell Bryan

guarantee all the liabilities of the entire system: $16 trillion dollars or whatever it's been.

The reason I marvel is that we don't know if this is going to be effective or not. We're on a new course here. We have no idea what may come out the other end, in terms of potential inflation, double dips, the role of the US economy, the value of the dollar. We are undertaking as quick a fix as possible of something that took years and years to build up.

There's one of two outcomes from this. One is that the quick fix will work but not fix the fundamentals. And then I'm really concerned, because I don't think we'll have a foundation for good, sound growth. The other is that no matter what we do, we're going to have a deep recession, which will give us time to fix the system—and we *will* fix the system. We will get leverage down to good levels. We will deal with our trade imbalances. And strategists and their companies will learn how to get by in this environment.

What I'm most worried about now is that we may think it's over before it's over. Because if we don't fix things that have gotten excessive and we've used up all of our gunpowder, it could be really ugly in about three or four years, as we do a big double dip or inflation gets out of control.

Richard Rumelt

Richard Rumelt: As Lowell pointed out, it's been a surprisingly vigorous response, and we don't know if it's going to work. Spending money may or may not stimulate the economy. Quantitative easing may or may not stimulate the economy. There's no certainty. The empirical evidence is very, very mixed. The Keynesians will tell you that the Depression was fixed by the spending on the Second World War. But that's really a misreading of history.

What happened during the Second World War was that ten million Americans were put into indentured military service at minimum wage. Consumers endured rationing. And the government rebuilt the industrial infrastructure with cost-plus contracts. After the war was won, it turned out that household balance sheets had been restructured back to almost zero debt. There was this huge pent-up demand to buy anything. And people went back to work at real salaries. To repeat that today, you'd have to take the ten million employees in financial services, draft them into some kind of Peace Corps, and have them rebuild the highways for four years, at minimum wage. It's an appealing prospect. But the sanctity of their bonus contracts probably prevents it.

The Quarterly: *Is the policy response helping or hindering the reallocation of resources in the private sector?*

Richard Rumelt: Mostly, it hinders. The real economy boils down to what work people do. I believe we are now in a structural break and that the mix of work being done has to change. If things go right, we will find, in five years, that we are, on the whole, doing a lot less of some activities, and more of others. In my view, a good policy response helps individuals defray the costs of the shift. If you're an auto worker, it's not your fault. On the other hand, if we act to prevent the shift, if we prop up the institutions that have declined, that becomes a problem. If we start creating zombie car companies and zombie banks that are essentially propped up by the government, that's a problem.

> 'If we start creating zombie car companies and zombie banks that are essentially propped up by the government, that's a problem'

The worst policy is to prop up people in jobs that are no longer necessary. The right policy, I think, is some balance where you help people deal with the costs of changes in employment rather than have the costs all privatized, which isn't really fair, because someone's benefitting from the change and someone's losing. And very often, the employees aren't at fault—they're just part of the system and they ought to be helped. But they should be helped in a way other than guaranteeing them jobs doing what doesn't need to be done.

Lowell Bryan: I think there's a potential that we go down the path of trying to protect people, and in the process we put in a lot more rigidities that make us fundamentally less effective at innovation. That migrates to Asia and we, basically, go down the European path. That would be sad for us and the world. But that's a possibility. That's one of the scenarios about how this plays out: we become a safer, poorer place, with less change.

One of the interesting things I see, which is probably a healthy and good response, is government-funded R&D: things like clean energy, health care. Obviously, the military keeps doing R&D too. Behind an awful lot of the raw innovation that takes place, you'll find some

Globalization and its discontents

Rik Kirkland

The financial crisis and resulting recession have focused attention on the rise of protectionism, the US social safety net, and what it affords those who have lost their jobs. Matthew Slaughter, a professor of international trade at Dartmouth's Tuck School of Business and a member of the US Council of Economic Advisers from 2005 to 2007, and Richard Haass, the president of the Council on Foreign Relations, offered their views on these topics in recent but separate interviews with McKinsey's Rik Kirkland. Edited excerpts follow.

The *Quarterly*: *If you were in the current administration, would you be advising it not to support a bailout of General Motors?*

Matthew Slaughter: I've given congressional testimony on this question and said I really want to support the workers at companies like General Motors and the communities where they operate. I don't want to support GM as a company directly, using taxpayer dollars.

It's much more important to think about expanding the social safety net. You look at the geographic concentration where GM and related suppliers are located—states like Michigan, Indiana, Ohio. There are a lot of struggling communities where we could take taxpayer dollars and allocate them to income support, worker retraining, and relocation, to the extent that the best option for some folks is moving to another community or another state. That is a better use of taxpayer dollars and allows the aggregate productivity gains that have been so important, not just in autos but in every industry in the US, to support rising standards of living.

In part, the United States has been able to grow for many decades by having struggling companies shrink if they need to shrink. The government does have an important role to play, again, through the social safety net, but we're moving away from that right now in the United States and in a lot of other countries. And it's not quite clear where we're going to end up.

The *Quarterly*: *There seems to be a swing away from the post–Second World War consensus on free trade. How serious is that?*

Richard Haass: There is a move away from free trade toward protectionism. These things go in cycles. This is a powerful one now, and it's not surprising. It was already happening because Americans were concerned about globalization and its challenges. And then on top of that, now you have a recession, where people are losing jobs or fearful about losing jobs, for good reason. So it doesn't come as any surprise that, in this context, the forces of protection have gained.

But there are all sorts of reasons to fight back. Trade is the best noninflationary stimulus I can think of. It's also got a useful political dimension—it's a way to give countries a stake in one another's well being. It gives countries a stake in peace because they understand that they don't want to disrupt profitable trade.

So the challenge is to rebuild a political consensus—say, in the United States—in favor of open trade. This means getting the arguments out there. But even more, it means cushioning workers so that they come to the conclusion that, yes, while they will be buffeted by globalization, they have the education tools, the training tools, the health care tools, what have you, not simply to survive globalization but to thrive in it.

Rik Kirkland is McKinsey's director of publishing.

government program that's invented something or caused something to be invented. Now, a lot of the R&D doesn't help for a decade or more. But I think that's an area where the government could help—just get the raw engine of research going.

The Quarterly: *How worried are you about a backlash that undermines the global system?*

Richard Rumelt: There's an enormous amount of pent-up political anger that currently isn't being expressed because everybody is afraid that if you get too angry, one of these banks may keel over and die, and then we're back in the soup, as with Lehman Brothers. It's a very delicate and emotional political balance right now—you have institutions that are taking enormous amounts of resources and basically threatening everybody with their imminent failure in order to garner more resources. That has to be fixed. We can't run a world economy with that kind of a relationship.

Lowell Bryan: I'm a little more sympathetic to the people currently in charge of most of these financial institutions, because—not entirely, but for the most part—these people are feeling a lot of anger as a result of things that were done by their predecessors.

Richard Rumelt: Fair enough. It's people playing roles they are inheriting. But the history of depressions and significant downturns shows us that they produce political results that are very long-lasting. Look at the 1873 collapse and what happened in Europe after that. The rise of anti-Semitism and, eventually, Nazism comes out of this. And that's the risk here—we get some fundamental political outgrowth that's dysfunctional.

Lowell Bryan: My biggest worry is a quick fix leading to inflation, so that by 2011 the Federal Reserve is in a dilemma—either to let inflation get out of control, with all the adverse effects to the currency, or to tighten up and put us into a double-dip recession. If we have rip-roaring inflation, the problem is that all the people who are holding dollars as instruments of wealth say, "You just bagged us." That can create enormous anger and it's quite a real possibility.

But I think the more likely scenario is that we'll go through a deep recession, that we'll get through it battered but remain resilient. I do think there's a fair chance that we will fix the

This conversation is one of three installments summarizing the reflections of Lowell Bryan and Richard Rumelt on the implications of the financial crisis. Read the full versions online at mckinseyquarterly.com.

credit system, fix the capital markets and that global expansion and global integration will resume. I would say that's more likely than the other scenario I gave you. But they're both out there. And we really are going to depend upon a lot of good policy and a little bit of luck to get us through this.

Richard Rumelt: I agree. I think the problems can be fixed. What the government needs to do—and only the government can do this—is to make decisions about who's going to take the hit. Somebody is going to be worse off here, and right now it looks like the taxpayer. But there are bond holders, there are various equity holders, there are many, many, many interests out there, including national governments and sovereign funds. The system is frozen by the uncertainty about who's going to be left standing when everybody else has a seat. That uncertainty has to be resolved to get the global system working again.

The Quarterly: *Where do you think regulation of the financial system is headed?*

Richard Rumelt: Look, I've been a consultant to a lot of financial-services firms. They don't want to hear this, but there's a wide range of financial services—such as deposit taking, term life insurance, and life annuities—that should be utilities. They should be like gas and electricity. When companies compete in these products, it leads either to wild complexity or to risk taking that's simply not in keeping with the buyer's needs. You don't want companies that sell you electricity taking wild risks, and you don't want to invest your life savings in an annuity and then have that firm go belly up when you're 80 years old because it took some risk. All those kinds of financial services need to be like utilities. Competition in this area is oddly unstable. Firms compete, basically, by changing their credit standards. There have been cycles in both banking and insurance for centuries because of this.

'The biggest problem from 1997 on was not that we didn't have enough regulation; it's that we didn't have anybody enforcing the regulation we had'

Lowell Bryan: I'm not quite all the way where Richard is. I grew up in a financial-services industry that was highly regulated, and it was a little slow moving. I see a lot of benefits that occurred from the risk taking, from the innovation, and from this global capital market that we created, which fueled globalization and the integration of economies.

If you look at securitization from the 1970s until roughly 2000, you see mostly benefits from it. The reason it became unsound is that we allowed too much credit risk to enter the system. Prior to 2000, either the credit risks were assumed by the originator, or the borrower put up so much collateral or equity that no raw credit risk was allowed to pass through to the marketplace.

Related articles on mckinseyquarterly.com
Managing regulation in a new era
Asia's future and the financial crisis
A political education for business: An interview with the head of the Council on Foreign Relations

I would argue that the biggest problem from 1997 on was not that we didn't have enough regulation. It's that we didn't have anybody enforcing the regulation we had. There was plenty of power—in the SEC, Freddie Mac's and Fannie Mae's regulators, the banking system—to regulate a lot of this stuff. You didn't need new powers. What you did need was people intent on making the market work better, as opposed to basically regulating for the short-term benefit of the industry participants.

When you read the stories of what went on in the early 2000s, it was awful. People in charge of regulatory structures basically chose not to regulate. So I believe that this was a man-made disaster. If you're dealing with a nuclear power station and you take out all the rods that control the temperature of the reactor, you're going to have a blowup. And, frankly, we just took out all the rods until we had a blowup.

I'm concerned that we will go back to an overregulated, safe, dull, and slow-growing system. I think we need to find something between the regulation we had in the '60s and '70s—and the lack of regulation we had in the last decade. o

Copyright © 2009 McKinsey & Company. All rights reserved.

We welcome your comments on this article. Please send them to quarterly_comments@mckinsey.com.

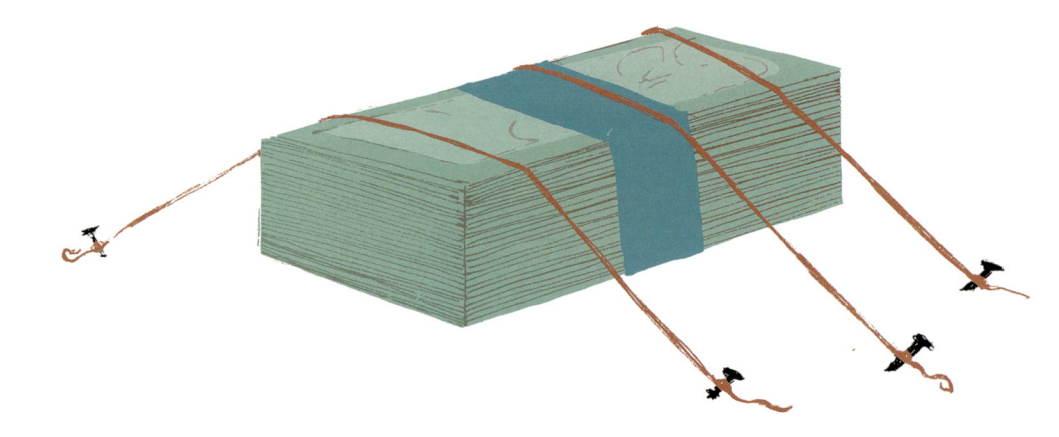

Learning from financial regulation's mistakes

Current bank oversight failed to prevent the financial crisis. Let's not prescribe more of the same.

Patrick Butler

The G-20 meeting in London earlier this year set the direction for reforming the regulation of financial services to prevent a recurrence of the present crisis. Still to come is the hard work of hammering out the details, which will determine if a new regulatory system can succeed—without imposing excessive costs or triggering unintended consequences.

The causes of the current crisis resemble those of many previous ones: banks that didn't have enough capital lent too much, too easily, relying on wholesale funding that disappeared when the inevitable concerns about asset quality arose. Yet there are important differences this time. The current problem started in what were regarded as the world's safest and most sophisticated markets and spread globally, carried by securities and derivatives that were thought to make the financial system safer.

If regulators working on solutions resist the reflex to build incrementally on conventional wisdom and existing structures, we now have an opportunity to reshape the global regulatory system fundamentally. That will require a dispassionate assessment of the reasons for the current system's failure. The difficult issues regulators must address include the appropriate degree of protection for financial institutions, the regulation of nonbank entities (such as hedge funds), and the determination of adequate capital levels. Brave—even radical— changes may be necessary.

Patrick Butler is a director in McKinsey's London office.

Tackling 'too big to fail'
A large bank's failure poses risks to other institutions, the financial system, and the broader economy. For this reason, regulators often step in to protect not only the bank's depositors but also all its creditors (and sometimes shareholders) from losses they would otherwise face. Banks for which governments are likely to intervene are seen as "too big to fail" (TBTF). While this kind of protection solves the immediate problem, it increases longer-term systemic risk because creditors or investors have less reason to monitor banks they see as TBTF, and the managers of these banks have a greater incentive to take risks. Governments tried to mitigate this element of moral hazard by being deliberately ambiguous about which banks they would rescue and on what terms, but the recent rescues obliterated this ambiguity, and the world now believes that no large financial institution—bank or nonbank—will be allowed to fail in the way nonfinancial companies do.

Most proposals to address the TBTF problem, from the G-20 and others, recommend regulating and supervising large, complex financial institutions more tightly. Yet the clear message of economic history is that incentives overpower regulation. Measures are needed to prevent, or at least discourage, institutions from becoming too big to fail in the first place and to wind them down if they do. Several actions could be taken to prevent them from becoming so big that they create systemic risks. It may be possible to use antitrust approaches originally designed to prevent markets from becoming too concentrated. Additional capital charges or insurance fees on institutions could be levied in proportion to the level of systemic risk they pose—in effect, charging them a market price for the TBTF guarantee. Stronger national-level regulation of the subsidiaries and branches of international banks could ensure that the impact of their failure was contained. Finally, investment banking and commercial banking could be kept more separate than they are now.

Besides prevention, we need a cure—a system for liquidating large banks in a way that controls systemic risk but still ensures that investors, creditors, and managers bear sufficient pain to eradicate moral hazard. The United States has a tried-and-tested bank wind-down process, but it is designed for straightforward domestic commercial banking and would need to be adapted for more complex and global institutions. Lessons from the troubles of AIG and Lehman Brothers could help to design such a process. Creative ideas have been proposed for handling failures by immediately transferring good assets to a new, smaller but shiny "bridge bank." That would leave uninsured creditors with not only a "bad bank" holding troubled assets but also some equity in the new institution.[1]

It is not clear whether governments coping with the present crisis were right to rescue and continue to support so many banks. But incentives

---

[1] See, for instance, Jeremy Bulow and Paul Klemperer, *Reorganising the banks: Focus on the liabilities, not the assets*, VoxEU.org, March 21, 2009.

matter: no matter how big banks are regulated, there will be many more failures if they always expect to be bailed out.

Mitigating universal-bank risks
Conducting commercial- and investment-banking activities in a single institution is a variant of the TBTF problem, but one that requires its own remedies. Commercial and investment banks have different risk profiles. Commercial banks create credit vital to the real economy yet are inherently fragile: if all depositors want their money back at the same time, any bank will go broke. Governments therefore insure retail depositors, central banks act as lenders of last resort, and banks submit to regulation, supervision, and the maintenance of minimum levels of capital. Investment banks too support the economy by helping companies raise capital and maintaining liquidity. But to do so, these institutions trade actively in the capital markets, where bubbles and crashes are endemic and, as a result, the rewards and risks are commensurately bigger than those of commercial banks.

There are economic advantages to be had from combining commercial and investment banks, and the prevailing wisdom has been that any risks from doing so can be controlled. The current crisis has presented no evidence that combined (or "universal") banks are more vulnerable or blameworthy than pure investment or pure commercial ones. But the crucial point is that combining the two kinds of institutions extended the protection given to commercial banks to investment banking, artificially reducing its cost of capital. That encouraged the growth of larger, more complex institutions and transferred to taxpayers costs and risks that no one had contemplated.

Ignoring this downside would be a mistake, as would peremptory regulation to separate investment and commercial banking. We need a balanced reappraisal of the advantages and disadvantages of universal banking. Even if there is no justification for untangling commercial- and investment-banking activities, stronger firewalls may be required between them, at least for deposit insurance and government guarantees.

Regulating nonbanks
One thrust of the G-20 agenda is the extension of regulatory oversight to institutions in what has become known as the "shadow banking system," such as hedge funds, private-equity funds, insurance companies, and off-balance-sheet vehicles. Such moves are undoubtedly necessary but should be made cautiously.

First, regulation imposes real costs on society. In particular, prudential regulation creates anticompetitive economies of scale, impairs innovation, adds costs, helps preserve weak management and business models, and passes the pain on to taxpayers if institutions falter. Second, few if any hedge and private-equity funds actually present systemic risk. The unique feature of banks (and some of their off-balance-sheet vehicles) is that many of their liabilities must be repaid on demand and that any failure to do so has a falling-domino effect. Virtually all other financial institutions, by contrast, tend to borrow for a specific term or against collateral. If they fail, investors and creditors lose money but not immediate access to cash. For this reason, the same level of supervision and regulation is not appropriate for both categories of institutions.

Finally, it is debatable whether regulation actually makes institutions safer or sounder. Markets, not regulators, first identified and acted upon the problems in the present crisis, and the failure rate of regulated institutions isn't clearly lower than that of unregulated ones: Citigroup, after all, is probably the most heavily regulated and supervised institution on the planet. The current safety-and-soundness regulation of commercial banks has failed. Proposals for other kinds of institutions must take into account both their different risk profiles and the shortcomings of the way commercial banks are regulated.

Improving product transparency
So far, proposals for managing systemic risk lean toward a more vigilant monitoring of the global financial system and tighter supervision of institutions deemed systemically important. What is also needed is a much better understanding of how systemic risk develops and spreads. It may well be that risk is caused as much by products as by institutions.

At the heart of the current crisis were a clutch of products carrying opaque three-letter acronyms, such as ABS, CDO, CLO, SIV, and CDS. Neither the people who designed these products nor their purchasers fully understood them. Yet they poisoned the financial system, spreading silently but virally across the globe, mutating as they went, and reaching system-threatening size without attracting attention. Regulators have resisted interfering in the development or dissemination of these products, fearing that doing so would dampen the dynamism of capital markets. Yet much so-called innovation is aimed more at exploiting loopholes and skirting regulation than at meeting the needs of customers. Products of this kind are unnecessarily—deliberately—complex and opaque. The world of finance, as the economist John Kenneth Galbraith noted, "hails the invention of the wheel over and over again, often in a slightly more unstable form."

Controls on product innovation don't stifle other industries with potentially dangerous products. Pharmaceutical companies, for instance, can't sell products—even to professional buyers—until they are rigorously tested and the trial results become available.

Perhaps the best way to manage the financial sector's systemic risk is to put a brake on its carriers and require all products over a certain volume to be traded on an exchange rather than over the counter or, at a minimum, to create a mandatory central clearing house for them. This approach would make products simpler, more standardized, and more transparent, reducing the latent liquidity and counterparty risks that come to the fore in financial crises.

Determining 'adequate capital'
By common consent, banks should hold more capital. How much and in what form are less straightforward questions. More capital makes the industry safer but also lowers returns and, by extension, probably raises prices for customers. It is critical to balance the need to control risks with the need for attractive returns.

Many proposals to strike that balance are encouraging. There is general agreement, for instance, that capital levels should be set counter-cyclically—in other words, institutions should build up higher levels in good times to form a bigger buffer in recessions. There are also ideas to complement the conventional risk-weighted capital targets with limits on leverage (assets divided by equity). Two metrics, whatever their individual merits, are better than one, since asking a bank to optimize on a single metric invites unproductive regulatory arbitrage.

Some proposals to replace the underlying risk models used to calculate capital are a matter of concern. The existing models, sophisticated as they are, couldn't cope with the multiplicity of risks in the financial system—they underestimated counterparty, liquidity, and market risk, as well as the risk of rare, so-called Black Swan events. Consultants, academics, and economists have suggested ways to make such models even more sophisticated. While internal risk management might benefit from these ideas, it is more important to make the models for setting regulatory capital easily understood, objective, and, as John Maynard Keynes put it, "vaguely right rather than precisely wrong."

The form of capital that banks should hold has been much less debated than the amount. Yet it may not be appropriate or efficient to carry equity capital against genuine "tail risk" (or extremely low-probability) events. After all, individuals don't put aside sums of money in case their houses are struck by lightning. What's more, when a bank suffers a sudden capital shock, it is very difficult to raise equity quickly, and the only real option is to sell assets, which in a nervous mark-to-market environment can weaken the capital ratios or collateral positions of other banks, creating a general fire-sale effect. What makes sense for a single bank is harmful for the system. We should explore how banks can protect themselves against tail risk by holding "contingent capital"—for instance, hybrid securities that start as debt and then convert automatically to equity if certain low-probability events occur.

Rethinking the supervision model
Regulating and supervising banks is difficult. Moreover, the greatest systemic risks occur in boom times, when the industry's political

support is strongest and oversight less popular. The answer is not just to hire additional regulators and pay them more. The model of supervision must be rethought fundamentally.

One possibility could be moving to enforcement based on rules rather than the prevailing "guidelines" approach. Particularly at the height of an economic boom, guidelines are very hard for regulators to enforce. In a system based on rules, the burden would be removed from regulators—for instance, if banks breached capital requirements, a set of previously agreed upon, nonnegotiable escalating responses could be triggered, starting at an earlier stage than they do today. They could include imposing tighter supervision, restricting dividends or bonus payments, or requiring debt-to-equity conversions until proper ratios were restored.

Another change of model could involve what Daniel Roth in *Wired* magazine called "radical transparency."[2] Financial institutions and other public companies now disclose their activities to investors after the fact, in lengthy reports that are neither granular nor synthesized enough to be insightful. Every year, the US Securities & Exchange Commission's public-document database, Edgar, catalogs 200 gigabytes of filings, roughly 15 million pages of text—up from 35 gigabytes a decade ago. Regulators have greater access to information about companies than investors do but are even more overwhelmed by complex data. Despite all this disclosure, when market liquidity dried up in late 2007, nobody knew what institutions held which toxic assets. Roth's proposal is to exploit the "wisdom of crowds" by forcing companies to report more detailed data, online, in real time, and—critically—uniformly tagged so they can be exported into spreadsheets for exploration and analysis. The massive, parallel-processing, and number-crunching power of curious, interested, and directly motivated people around the world would then undertake much of the supervision required.

Neither of these specific ideas may be right, but in the information age the supervision of a vital global industry should not depend on the herculean efforts of a few well-intentioned officials drowning in data and outnumbered and outgunned by profit-seeking bankers. The system can be smarter than that.

Achieving international cooperation
Financial markets have outgrown national boundaries and domestic regulatory systems, to the point where no nation can control its own fate. International claims on banks rose to $35 trillion last year, from $6 trillion in 1990. Massive flows take place not only in the well-understood international bond market but also in the interbank, securitization, derivatives, and cross-border-lending markets. Many of the

---

[2] See Daniel Roth, "Road map for financial recovery: Radical transparency now!" *Wired*, 2009, Volume 17, Issue 3.

effects are positive, but there is a high risk that problems will spread from country to country and that regulation's unforeseen consequences in one will have an impact on another.

For these reasons, global regulation and supervision remain many years away—a reality the G-20 recognized when it refrained from calling for a global regulator. Instead, it proposed the creation of national colleges of supervisors to develop regulatory rules and of a financial stability board, the successor to the Financial Stability Forum (FSF), to monitor the global financial system and make recommendations to regulators and national governments. Pragmatic and quick agreement is needed to make this kind of cooperation work—for example, to decide how the colleges of supervisors will together develop common solutions and how individual countries will adopt them.

There must also be an honest debate about why existing monitors of systemic risk—the International Monetary Fund and the FSF—failed in their task. Were they unable to see the risk until it was too late, or were alarm bells drowned out by the bull market's euphoria? Either way, changing the name of the FSF and exhorting it to be more vigilant or vocal will accomplish little. We need to decide if it needs greater scope to detect potential crises, more teeth, or both. Finally, despite fears of economic nationalism, there may be a need for greater regulation and supervision of foreign subsidiaries and branches by host countries until genuinely international regulation emerges. Few if any of the new regulations suggested for banks can be imposed in some large countries but not in others without triggering massive and counterproductive arbitrage. The mechanics of coordination and cooperation must be determined quickly.

Related articles on mckinseyquarterly.com
What's next for US banks
Surveying the economic horizon: A conversation with Robert Shiller
Regulation that's good for competition

• • •

A once-in-a-generation opportunity to redesign the global financial system is at hand. The broad direction of reform is clear, but the details are important and getting them wrong will prepare the way for the next financial failure. The design of reform should be careful and deliberate, based on a thorough analysis of the underlying problems. It should be sufficiently creative and innovative to provide solutions for the next 20 years instead of revising approaches that haven't worked for the past 20. And it should tackle issues that are difficult politically, such as the protection of TBTF institutions.

Rebuilding corporate reputations

A perfect storm has hit the standing of big business. Companies must step up their reputation-management efforts in response.

Sheila Bonini, David Court, and Alberto Marchi

Sheila Bonini is a consultant in McKinsey's Silicon Valley office, **David Court** is a director in the Dallas office, and **Alberto Marchi** is a director in the Milan office.

As governments respond to the financial crisis and its reverberations in the real economy, a company's reputation has begun to matter more now than it has in decades. Companies and industries with reputation problems are more likely to incur the wrath of legislators, regulators, and the public. What's more, the credibility of the private sector will influence its ability to weigh in on contentious issues, such as protectionism, that have serious implications for the global economy's future.

Senior executives are acutely aware of how serious today's reputational challenge is. Most recognize the perception that some companies in certain sectors (particularly financial services) have violated their social contract with consumers, shareholders, regulators, and taxpayers. They also know that this perception seems to have spilled over to business more broadly. In a March 2009 *McKinsey Quarterly* survey of senior executives around the world, 85 and 72 percent of them, respectively, said that public trust in business and commitment to free markets had deteriorated.[1] According to the 2009 Edelman Trust Barometer, those executives are reading the public mind correctly: 62 percent of respondents, across 20 countries, say that they "trust corporations less now than they did a year ago."

[1] See "Economic Conditions Snapshot, March 2009: McKinsey Global Survey Results," mckinseyquarterly.com, March 2009.

The breadth and depth of today's reputational challenge is a consequence not just of the speed, severity, and unexpectedness of recent economic events but also of underlying shifts in the reputation environment that have been under way for some time. Those changes include the growing importance of Web-based participatory media, the increasing significance of nongovernmental organizations (NGOs) and other third parties, and declining trust in advertising. Together, these forces are promoting wider, faster scrutiny of companies and rendering traditional public-relations tools less effective in addressing reputational challenges.

Now more than ever, it will be action—not spin—that builds strong reputations. Organizations need to enhance their listening skills so that they are sufficiently aware of emerging issues; to reinvigorate their understanding of, and relationships with, critical stakeholders; and to go beyond traditional PR by activating a network of supporters who can influence key constituencies. Doing so effectively means stepping up both the sophistication and the internal coordination of reputation efforts. Some companies, for example, not only use cutting-edge attitudinal-segmentation techniques to better understand the concerns of stakeholders but also mobilize cross-functional teams to gather intelligence and respond quickly to far-flung reputational threats.

One key to cutting through organizational barriers that might impede such efforts is committed senior leadership, including from CEOs, who have an opportunity in today's charged environment to differentiate their companies by demonstrating real statesmanship. The stakes demand it; an energized public will expect nothing else.

A rapidly evolving reputation environment

The financial crisis has underscored just how ill-equipped companies can be to deal with two important changes in the reputation environment. First, the influence of indirect stakeholders—such as NGOs, community activists, and online networks—has grown enormously. These proliferating indirect stakeholders have tasked business with a broader set of expectations, such as making globalization more humane and combating climate change, obesity, human-rights abuses, or HIV.

An interview with two 'reputation gurus'—Stanley Greenberg and Howard Paster—is available as a sidebar to this article on mckinseyquarterly.com.

Second, the proliferation of media technologies and outlets, along with the emergence of new Web-based platforms, has given individuals and organizations new tools they use to subject companies to greater and faster scrutiny. This communications revolution also means that certain issues (such as poor labor conditions) that might be acceptable in one region can be picked up by "citizen journalists" or bloggers and generate outrage in another.

As a result, what formerly were operational risks resulting from failed or inadequate processes, people, or systems now often manifest themselves as reputational risks whose costs far exceed those of the original missteps. In banking, for example, data privacy has become a reputational issue. In pharmaceutical clinical trials, Merck's experience with Vioxx showed that anything less than full transparency can lead to disaster. And as risk-management problems in the financial sector have generated astronomical losses that taxpayers are helping bear, it's little wonder that the reputational fallout has been enormous.

An outmoded approach to reputation management
In this dispersed and multifaceted environment, companies must collect information about reputational threats across the organization, analyze that information in sophisticated ways, and address problems by taking action to mitigate them. That can involve developing alliances with new kinds of partners and coordinating responses from a number of parties, including governments, civil-society groups, and consumers. All this requires significant coordination and an ability to act quickly.

Many companies, though, rely primarily on small, central corporate-affairs departments that can't monitor or examine diverse reputational threats with sufficient sophistication. Moreover, traditional PR spin can't deal with many NGO concerns, which must often be addressed by changing business operations and conducting two-way conversations. Managers of business units have a better position for spotting potential challenges but often fail to recognize their reputational significance. Internal communication about them may be inhibited by the absence of consistent methodologies for tracking and quantifying reputational risk. Accountability for managing problems is often blurred.

As a result, responses to reputational issues can be short term, ad hoc, and defensive—a poor combination today given the intensity of public concern. And therein lies a problem that companies must solve quickly: even as reputational challenges boost the importance of good PR, companies will struggle if they rely on PR alone, with little insight into the root causes of or the facts behind their reputational problems.

A better, more integrated response
A logical starting point for companies seeking to raise their game is to put in place an effective early-warning system to make executives aware of reputational problems quickly. In our experience, most companies are quite good at tracking press mentions, and many are

beginning to monitor the multitude of Web-based voices and NGOs, whose power is beginning to rival the mainstream media's. However, doing these things effectively, while an important prerequisite for stepping up engagement with stakeholders, isn't the toughest task facing organizations.

Far more of a challenge is preparing to meet serious reputational threats, whose potential frequency and cost have risen dramatically given the greater likelihood that stakeholders—including regulators and legislators—will lash out in an atmosphere that's become less hospitable to business. These threats might take a variety of forms: issues related to a company's business performance, like those that financial companies have recently experienced; unexpected shocks along the lines of Johnson & Johnson's Tylenol scare, more than two decades ago; opposition to business moves, such as expanding operations; or long-standing, sector-specific issues, for instance climate change (industrials and oil and gas), obesity (the food and beverage industry), hidden fees (telecom providers), "e-waste" (high tech), and worker safety (mining).

To prepare for and respond to these threats, our experience suggests that companies should emphasize three priorities. First, they need to assemble enough facts—most important, perhaps, a rich understanding of key stakeholders, including consumers—and not only the product preferences but also the political attitudes of consumer groups. Second, companies should focus on the actions that matter most to stakeholders, something that may call for an exaggerated degree of transparency about corporate priorities or operations. Third, they must try to influence stakeholders through techniques that go beyond traditional PR approaches, with an emphasis on two-way dialogue. Underlying these priorities is a willingness to participate in the public debate more actively than many companies have in the past. Instead of allowing single-issue interest groups to control the conversation, companies should insist on a more complete dialogue that raises awareness of the difficult trade-offs they face.

Understanding stakeholders and their concerns
Companies should first develop a deeper understanding of the reputational issues that matter to their stakeholders and of the degree to which their products, services, operations, supply chains, and other activities affect those issues. A company trying to improve its environmental reputation, for example, needs to document, catalog, and assess its sustainability efforts and then to benchmark them against those of its competitors and industry standards. The facts should be presented objectively and, if possible, quantitatively—for example, the amount of carbon emitted or water used. Quantitative measurements promote effective comparisons and help companies avoid ignoring potential issues or performance gaps.

Such an analysis may lead a company to conclude that it has a good story that should be told more vigorously—or that it should refrain from doing so until it takes real action. The analysis also is the starting point for an objective quantification of reputational risks. The company can prioritize them and the measures needed to keep them at bay by assessing the probability and financial cost of potential reputational events, such as consumer boycotts or the forced closure of operations.

Reputations are built on perceptions, however, so issue analysis isn't enough. Companies must also know if they are meeting the expectations of key stakeholders—those in the best position to influence sales and growth. To identify these centers of influence, companies should cast a wide net, scrutinizing not just traditional stakeholders (consumers, employees, shareholders, and regulators) but also indirect ones, such as NGOs and the media, that help shape attitudes. Even for companies that don't deal directly with consumers, it's important to understand public opinion. People have unprecedented access to information now and may therefore concern themselves with a surprisingly wide array of issues, potentially providing the impetus for regulatory or legislative action.

Each kind of stakeholder has unique perceptions and concerns. Shareholders might ask if reputational issues will affect a company's long-term growth prospects. Regulators could worry that the public thinks they should curb the company. The media might wonder if it could be an example of how business exploits society. There are different ways of identifying the perceptions of each kind of stakeholder and their root causes (Exhibit 1). A detailed press analysis can help companies to understand the positions of columnists and editors on key issues. Interviews with regulators can clarify their concerns. Focus groups and market research are important for understanding consumers and the wider public.

If consumer research is required, companies must understand that an analysis of how different consumers feel about them differs from typical segmentations: one for reputation management resembles a dissection of voters in a political campaign rather than a parsing of customers who prefer different types of products or services. There might, for example, be a group of consumers who care deeply about social issues and will weigh in aggressively on regulatory ones affecting a company's operations. Others, such as swing voters, might be undecided about whether, or how, to become involved. Some could be uninterested and unlikely to take action. Still others may be so anti- or probusiness that their positions are set in stone. One consumer company facing regulatory challenges used this type of "social attitudinal" segmentation to analyze consumers (Exhibit 2). After identifying people who were both influential and open-minded, the company

Exhibit 1

Understanding the stakeholders

A company can employ methods specific to each type of stakeholder in seeking to understand its position on reputational issues.

	Consumers and partners	Media, including Internet, newspapers, TV	Shareholders, analysts, investors	Regulators	Civil society—eg, activist groups, nongovernmental organizations (NGOs), labor unions
Key issues	• Avoiding purchases, because of negative perceptions of company	• Portraying big business issues in a negative light • Lacking the in-depth reporting required for a balanced view of the issue	• Effect on share prices • Changing investments	• Shaping policy and regulation • Monitoring impact on consumers, environment, and society	• Advocating environmental, social, governance, and economic standards
Key questions asked by stakeholders	• Limited; if any, probably through investment conferences	• Limited, usually through telephone discussions with investor relations unit	• Multiple in-depth meetings with executives at all senior leadership levels • Follow-up conversations, if necessary, with investor relations unit	• Occasional meetings, calls with investor relations unit • Semiannual or annual senior-management meetings	• Occasional meetings, calls with investor relations unit • Semiannual or annual senior-management meetings
Actions company can take	• Past financials, consensus estimates, trading information, implied valuation	• Web site, press releases, management press, sell-side analyst calls and reports, industry reports	• Past operations and unit-level information, management's future strategy and forecasts, industry outlook, management's background • Detailed follow-up information from company	• Quarterly updates on performance, significant changes in outlook	• Quarterly updates on performance, significant changes in outlook
Questions company should ask	• Limited; if any, probably through investment conferences	• Limited, usually through telephone discussions with investor relations unit	• Multiple in-depth meetings with executives at all senior leadership levels • Follow-up conversations, if necessary, with investor relations unit	• Occasional meetings, calls with investor relations unit • Semiannual or annual senior-management meetings	• Occasional meetings, calls with investor relations unit • Semiannual or annual senior-management meetings

focused on addressing their needs, and the public's attitudes toward it improved.

Transparency and action

Reputations are built on a foundation not only of communications but also of deeds: stakeholders can see through PR that isn't supported by real and consistent business activity. Consumers, our research indicates, feel that companies rely too much on lobbying and PR unsupported by action. They also fault companies for not sharing enough information about critical business issues—for manufacturers, say, the content of their products, their manufacturing processes, and their treatment of production employees. Transparency in such matters is crucial. Sometimes it highlights a mismatch between consumer expectations and a company's performance and therefore calls for action. In other cases, transparency can convince key stakeholders that the company is headed in the right direction.

After the director of the US Food and Drug Administration voiced reservations about the side effects of the high-cholesterol treatment Crestor, for example, AstraZeneca not only placed ads in the national press to present its case but also took the unusual step of providing raw clinical-trial data on its Web site, allowing completely independent researchers to draw their own conclusions. This was a high-risk strategy, since it's always possible to draw different statistical inferences from the same data. But the strategy reestablished public trust and stabilized Crestor's market share.

Consider also the efforts of the US plastics industry to overcome a consumer and regulatory backlash, in the late 1980s, over plastic packaging's environmental impact. The CEOs of leading companies joined forces to reframe the public debate not just through an award-winning ad campaign illustrating positive applications of plastics (in child safety, for example) but also by committing the industry to recycling and thus to solving environmental problems. The industry could do so credibly because it undertook real actions, such as spending $1.2 billion on recycling research and developing a standardized plastics-coding system.

Such actions need not take place only in response to reputational concerns; at other times, they help build goodwill that may provide some degree of cover against future bad news. A willingness to tackle climate change has helped companies like Toyota Motor and GE, for example, build strong reputations that are holding up better than those of many other major automotive and financial-services players. Sometimes, reputation-oriented actions may even have a direct impact on sales. In 2008, for instance, Best Buy began inviting customers to

---

Exhibit 2

Whom to target

For disguised European consumer company

Attitudinal segments

% of population

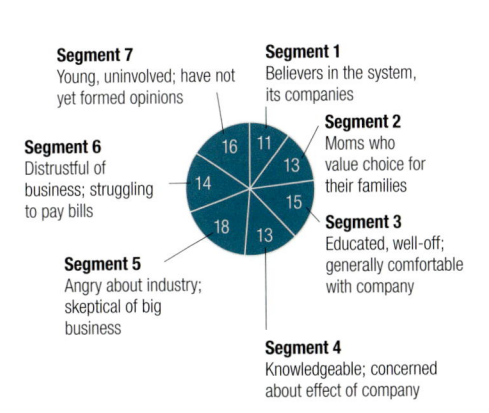

Segment 7
Young, uninvolved; have not yet formed opinions

Segment 6
Distrustful of business; struggling to pay bills

Segment 5
Angry about industry; skeptical of big business

Segment 1
Believers in the system, its companies

Segment 2
Moms who value choice for their families

Segment 3
Educated, well-off; generally comfortable with company

Segment 4
Knowledgeable; concerned about effect of company

Perception of company by segments

Size of the bubble = segment size

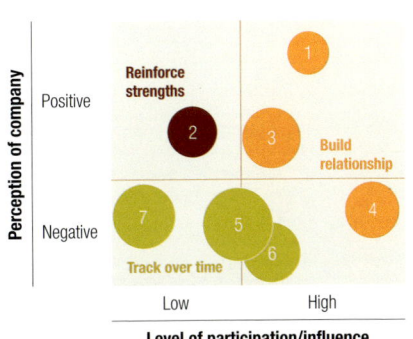

Perception of company: Positive / Negative
Level of participation/influence: Low / High

Reinforce strengths
Build relationship
Track over time

bring their old electronics into its stores for recycling. The program has not only generated positive press and helped position the company as an environmental leader but is also increasing foot traffic in stores.

Engaging a broad group of influencers

Formal marketing and PR do play an important role in managing the reputation of a company, but when it responds to serious threats it must use many other means of spreading positive messages about its activities quickly (Exhibit 3). In general, credible third parties speaking for the company can boost its reputation more effectively than its own PR or marketing department. Leveraging existing grassroots support—through blogs, bumper stickers, and interactive Web sites, for example—is one method. Another is to have people with high standing reinforce key strategic messages. Partnerships between the company and NGOs can be important not only because of their credibility but also because they can alert it to performance gaps early in the game. A network of positive relationships with credible third parties (such as journalists and NGOs) can also help the company get out its side of the story when crises do hit.

Exhibit 3

Tactics for influencing reputations

Using a number of communication channels, beyond the typical public-relations approach, can boost awareness of a company's activities effectively.

	Purpose	Examples	Desired outcomes
War room	To ensure opportunity to refute critics and deliver messages in daily news cycles	Media professionals' war room, responsible for monitoring, responding to news	No attack left unanswered; respond to every reporter
Free media	To deliver messages through low-cost, high-trust channels	Speeches, events, press conferences	Regularly create new stories showing company in favorable light
Paid media	To deliver messages with maximum control of message and targeting	Television, print ads, brochures, Web sites, mailings	Ensure everyone hears, sees, reads message
Networking	To develop relationships with broad set of stakeholders; listen and deliver messages to them	Meetings with politicians, organizations (eg, unions), media, other stakeholders	Wide network of influential supporters; better understanding of detractors
Giving	To reinforce messages through charitable contributions	Timberland's charitable focus on environmental causes	Positive associations from working on good causes
Operations	To reinforce messages and reduce reputational risks through activities within business	Starbucks's fair trade–certified coffee; Nike's supplier policies	Seamless integration between company's actions and reputational consequences
Partnerships	To gain credibility by working with others to solve industry-wide reputation issues	Labor certification standards in textile industry	More friends to help in shared reputation battles
Surrogates	To use high-credibility people to reinforce strategic messages	Placing prominent people on board, in executive positions	People with star power speaking up for the company
Grassroots	To leverage energy of current supporters	Bumper stickers, blogs, interactive Web sites	Support for company is highly visible

One company worried about what it saw as the dangerous inaccuracy of its portrayal in the press targeted opinion leaders with concise facts to dispel misunderstandings and gave regulators a scientific paper outlining the possible negative consequences of proposed regulations. A broader communication program describing recent and forthcoming changes in the company's business practices was released to the general public. This approach was effective, but even more nuanced forms of impact are possible: influencing specific bloggers, using company blogs to start conversations with consumers (a tactic Cisco, HP, and Intel, among others, use), and reaching scientists through research discussion boards.

Related articles on mckinseyquarterly.com
When social issues become strategic
The trust gap between consumers and corporations
Valuing corporate social responsibility

Increasingly, two-way dialogue is critical. Consider, for example, Chevron's "Will you join us?" campaign, which addresses many of the oil industry's most difficult questions, such as the developing world's energy needs, the role of renewables, environmental protection, and the problems that will get worse if we go on using oil as we do now. The campaign not only embodies a new level of openness about the industry's challenges but also asks the public to join the conversation on a Web site with a moderated discussion board and interactive tools providing information about conserving energy.

In this more complex world of influence strategy, no single kind of approach is likely to be sufficient to deal with fast-moving situations. Companies must instead initiate a multidisciplinary, cross-functional effort that can quickly identify reputational issues and plant responses in broader strategy, operations, and communications. The groups involved might include regulatory affairs, the general counsel, PR or corporate communications, marketing, corporate social responsibility, and investor relations.

To achieve the necessary coordination, a senior executive should be accountable for such efforts. A strong understanding of customers and marketing might make the CMO appropriate to play this role.[2] But it's the CEO who must lead a company's overall reputation strategy, ideally with the support of a board committee focused on it. This may seem like a lot of firepower, but in today's climate, with reputational issues threatening both shareholders and a company's ability to achieve broader goals, that degree of high-level attention and integration is essential.

Copyright © 2009 McKinsey & Company. All rights reserved.

We welcome your comments on this article. Please send them to quarterly_comments@mckinsey.com.

[2] See David Court, "The evolving role of the CMO," mckinseyquarterly.com, August 2007.

Center Stage
A look at current trends and topics in management

Squeezing more ideas from product teardowns

Dave Fedewa, Ashish Kothari, and Ananth S. Narayanan

Dave Fedewa and **Ashish Kothari** are consultants in McKinsey's Chicago office, where **Ananth Narayanan** is a principal.

Technophiles of all stripes love product teardowns—the time-honored practice of dismantling products to their constituent parts to spark fresh thinking. Yet few manufacturers get the full value teardowns afford. Many senior executives marginalize the practice, viewing teardowns as Skunk Works exercises for engineers or cost-cutting tactics on the part of the purchasing department. Such views retard creativity and ensure that the ideas generated in teardowns go unexplored, moldering in functional silos.

Not so for a medical-products company planning a series of teardowns to improve its therapeutic medical device. To foster new ideas, the company's senior executives invited purchasers, marketers, engineers, and sales personnel to see how their product stacked up against four rival ones.

Seeing the products together was an "Aha!" moment for the purchasers, who quickly identified a series of straightforward design changes that, while invisible to customers, would significantly lower the cost of manufacturing the device. Meanwhile, seeing the configurations of competitors' circuit boards spurred the team's salespeople, marketers, and engineers to discuss the manufacturing implications of the company's modular approach to design. The engineers had long assumed that being able to mix and match various features after final assembly was advantageous and had emphasized this capability in the product's design. Yet the salespeople reported that most customers hardly ever ordered more than a handful of modules at purchase and rarely ordered more after assembly. The conversations ultimately led to simplifications in the product's circuitry, which lowered purchasing costs by 23 percent and helped marketers identify a new customer segment where the product might command a higher price.

Elimination of metal base-plate on product's cart: 4 percent reduction in cost of cart

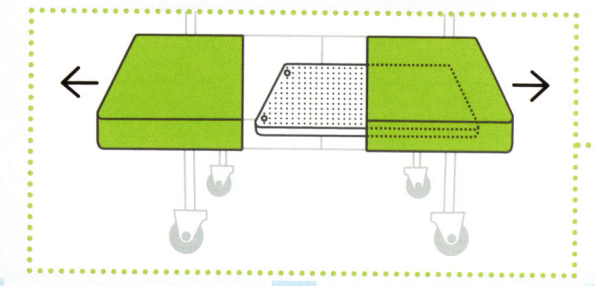

An interactive exhibit with examples from other industries is available on mckinseyquarterly.com.

85

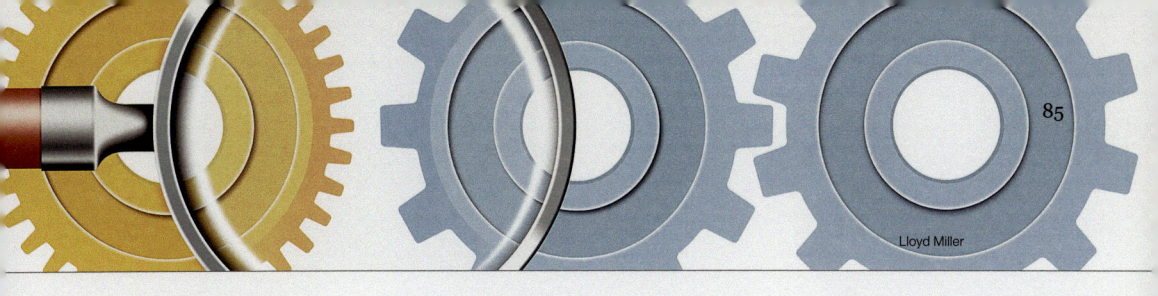

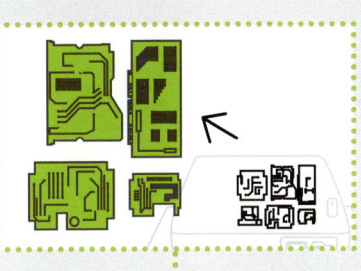

Lloyd Miller

Fewer printed circuit boards (PCB): 14 percent reduction in PCB cost

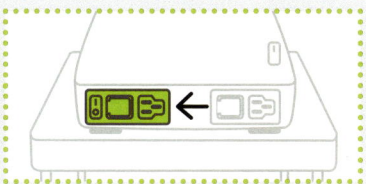

Integrated plug and fuse assembly: 12 percent cheaper; faster to assemble

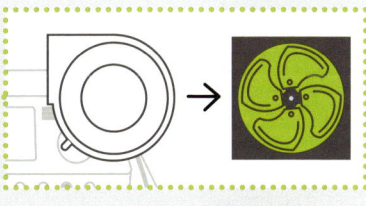

Changes in fan design from blower fan to box fan: 35 percent cheaper

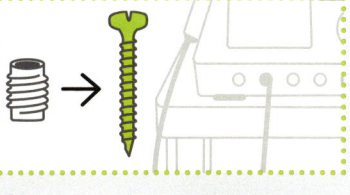

Self-tapping screws versus threaded inserts: 50 percent cheaper

Sophia Martineck

Energy, Resources, Materials

Electrifying cars: How three industries will evolve

Upon entering the mainstream—in a few years or a couple of decades—electrified cars will transform the auto and utilities sectors and create a new battery industry. What will it take to win in a battery-powered age?

Russell Hensley, Stefan Knupfer, and Dickon Pinner

It's a safe bet that consumers will eventually swap their gas-powered cars and trucks for rechargeable models. Electrified transport, in some form, would seem to be in our future. But how long will investors have to wait for the bet to pay off? Years? Decades?

Bears would bet on decades. For the next ten or so years, the purchase price of an electrified vehicle will probably exceed the price of an average gas-fueled family car by several thousand dollars. The difference is due largely to the cost of designing vehicles that can drive for extended distances on battery power and to the cost of the battery itself. What's more, the infrastructure for charging the batteries of a large number of electrified vehicles isn't in place, nor is the industry tooled to produce them on a mass scale. In any case, consumers aren't exactly clamoring for battery-powered sedans.

Bulls are betting on intervention by government. They think that concern over energy security, fossil fuel emissions, and long-term industrial competitiveness will prompt governments to seek a partial solution by creating incentives—some combination of subsidies, taxes, and investments—to migrate the market to battery-powered vehicles. In fact, governments across many regions are starting to act in this way. The bulls also note that electrified vehicles can address certain niches whose economics could be favorable more quickly, such as delivery and taxi fleets in large cities or elements of military fleets. In some countries, such as Israel, electrified vehicles already make economic

Russell Hensley is an associate principal and **Stefan Knupfer** is a director in McKinsey's Detroit office; **Dickon Pinner** is a principal in the San Francisco office.

sense because buyers get substantial tax breaks from the government. The bulls include innovators preparing new products and business models (such as the packaging of battery leasing and recharging costs) designed to make electrified vehicles more attractive to buyers.

Sooner or later, electrified vehicles will take off, changing several sectors profoundly. Let's assume that these vehicles will share the roads of the future with other low-carbon options, such as cars running on biofuels and vehicles with more fuel-efficient internal-combustion engines. Even then, significant sales of electrified vehicles could dramatically reshape the fortunes of the automotive and utilities sectors and propel the rise of a multibillion-dollar battery industry.

The stakes are high for companies in these industries. In the near term, executives should determine how to win revenues and contain costs if the governments of China and the United States, for example, live up to their promises to stimulate consumer purchases of electrified vehicles. Planning should also begin on strategies and on ways to build capabilities if early adoption creates a sustainable market.

Electrified vehicles: A glossary

The more conventional term "electric car" actually describes the all-electric sedan. But vehicles using electricity—*electrified vehicles*—actually come in a variety of forms.

Hybrid-electric vehicle
Such a vehicle has two or more energy storage systems, both of which must provide propulsion power, together or independently. The internal-combustion engine is typically the primary system, with the electric motor used to power the vehicle for short distances or to support the main engine— for example, when the vehicle idles at a stop light.

Plug-in hybrid-electric vehicle
These vehicles have one energy storage system: a battery recharged with power from either an on-board generating device (for example, a small internal-combustion engine) or an electricity supply into which the vehicle can be plugged.

Battery electric vehicle
This kind of vehicle has one energy storage system, a battery, and no primary on-board means of generating electricity. You transfer energy to the vehicle by plugging it into an electricity supply or by exchanging the battery for a charged one.

The green dream of electrified vehicles is more complicated than many realize. Visit mckinseyquarterly.com to read an online-only sidebar to this article, which discusses the emissions generated during fuel production for electrified vehicles.

Running on electrons

The economics of electrified vehicles start with the batteries, whose cost has been declining by 6 to 8 percent annually. Many analysts predict that it will continue to fall over the next ten years as production volumes rise (Exhibit 1). Battery packs now cost about $700 to $1,500 per kilowatt hour, but that could drop to as little as $420 per kilowatt hour by 2015 under an aggressive cost reduction scenario. Even then, the upfront purchase price of electrified cars would be quite high. We estimate that by 2015, a plug-in hybrid-electric vehicle with a battery range of 40 miles (before the need for a recharge) would initially cost $11,800 more than a standard car with a gas-fueled internal-combustion engine. A battery-powered electrified vehicle with a range of 100 miles would initially cost $24,100 more.

Subsidies could help bridge the difference. China announced that it will cover $8,800 of the cost of each electrified vehicle purchased by more than a dozen of its large-city governments and taxi fleets. Business innovation could address costs too. In the solar-technology market, for instance, SunEdison owns, finances, installs, operates, and maintains solar panels for customers willing to adopt the technology. The company then charges these consumers a predictable rate lower than

Exhibit 1

Learning curves

Lithium-ion battery cost assumptions,
$ per kilowatt hour (kWh), pack level

Projected breakthrough for materials and/or productivity, in addition to improvements in battery's state-of-charge window[1]

Scenarios
— High cost
— Medium cost
— Low cost

1,448

Learning curves not predictable in long term

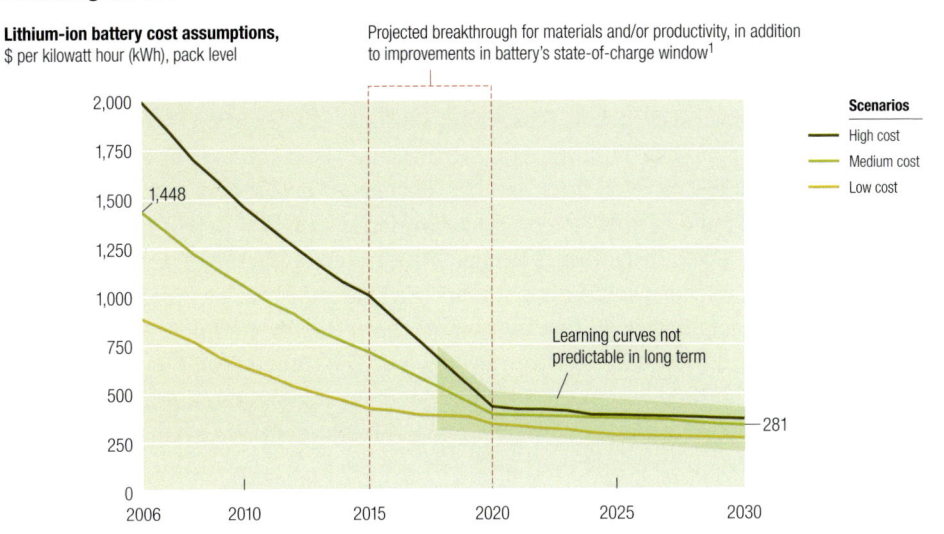

281

[1] State-of-charge window, is the available capacity in a battery relative to its capacity when full. Conservative applications work within a 65% window, whereas more aggressive applications use 80%; over the next 5 to 10 years, most applications will likely migrate to the higher value.

Source: OEM and supplier interviews conducted in Asia, Europe, and North America; McKinsey analysis

the one they paid for traditional electric power but higher than the actual cost of generation. That allows the company to recoup its capital outlay and make a profit.[1] Innovators are considering similar models to cover the battery's upfront cost and recoup the subsidy by charging for services.

To sway buyers, electrified vehicles—hybrids, plug-in electric hybrids, or all-electric cars (see "Electrified vehicles: A glossary")—must be cheaper to operate than gas-fueled ones. The difference between the total lifetime costs of a car with an internal-combustion engine and an electrified car will depend for some time on the difference between the price of gasoline at the pump and the cost of the battery and of recharging it (for those who own the battery) or the cost of leasing a battery and of recharging services. Oil prices have fluctuated wildly over the past two years, and electricity prices vary throughout the world. In Europe, electrified cars (for example, plug-in hybrid-electric vehicles with a 60-kilometer range) could have lower total running costs, assuming an oil price of $60 a barrel and current electric rates.[2] In the United States, electrified cars will be less expensive on a total-cost-of-ownership basis only if the price of gasoline exceeds $4 a gallon

[1] SunEdison's model also takes advantage of US state-level incentives for solar power.
[2] Clearly, this is a very conservative estimate. The McKinsey Global Institute estimates that energy demand will accelerate when the global economy rebounds, with a predictable impact on oil prices. For more, see MGI's full report, *Averting the next energy crisis: The demand challenge*, available free of charge on mckinsey.com/mgi.

and electric batteries can go 40 miles before a recharge, or if the government gives manufacturers incentives that subsidize the cost of production (Exhibit 2).

The proliferation of electrified vehicles will also require an infrastructure, such as recharging stations. China's State Grid is speeding up plans to build charging facilities in at least three of the country's largest cities by 2011, and the US state of Hawaii has announced plans to build as many as 100,000 charging stations for electrified vehicles by 2012. Investments in capabilities to manufacture the vehicles are needed as well. China, which set a goal of producing half a million electrified cars annually by 2011, has announced that it will invest $1.4 billion in R&D for the purpose. The United States has committed $2 billion in stimulus spending to help companies manufacture batteries and $25 billion for government programs to encourage car makers to retool their production lines to produce larger numbers of more fuel-efficient vehicles, including electrified ones.

Of course, consumers may decline to buy electrified vehicles for any number of reasons: the distance drivers can go before recharging, for example, may undermine acceptance. But on a more fundamental level, electrified vehicles will go mainstream at a pace determined by government action to make gasoline more expensive; to reduce the cost of producing, buying, or operating electrified vehicles; or some combination of these two approaches.

Preparing for tomorrow

There is little point in trying to predict how many electrified vehicles of one kind or other will be on the road by any given year, because

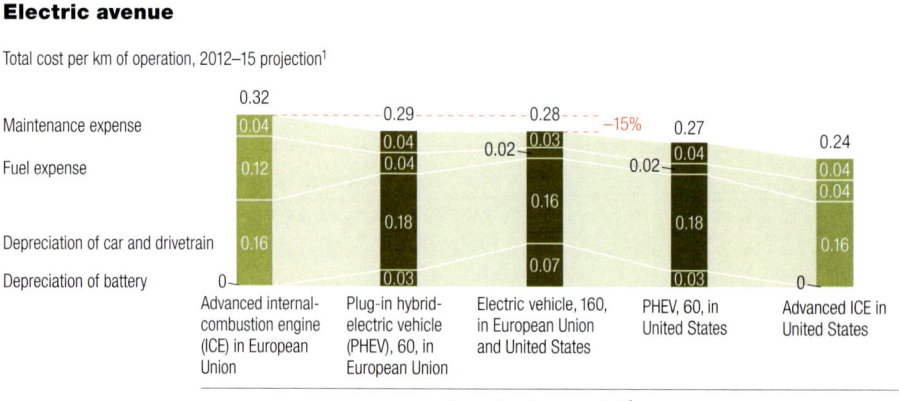

Exhibit 2

Electric avenue

Total cost per km of operation, 2012–15 projection[1]

Type of engine or vehicle[2]	Advanced internal-combustion engine (ICE) in European Union	Plug-in hybrid-electric vehicle (PHEV), 60, in European Union	Electric vehicle, 160, in European Union and United States	PHEV, 60, in United States	Advanced ICE in United States
Total	0.32	0.29	0.28	0.27	0.24
Maintenance expense	0.04	0.04	0.03	0.04	0.04
Fuel expense	0.12	0.04	0.02	0.02	0.04
Depreciation of car and drivetrain	0.16	0.18	0.16	0.18	0.16
Depreciation of battery	0	0.03	0.07	0.03	0

–15%

[1] Assumes fuel cost of $2.00 per gallon (United States), $1.69 per liter (European Union); battery pack cost of $500 per kilowatt hour (kWh); total cost of ownership calculated for first 5 years of ownership; 20,000 km per year annual distance driven; standard vehicle (eg, Volkswagen Golf) with cost of $20,000 before engine, drivetrain, battery, etc.; advanced ICE vehicle is 30% more efficient than 2008 Volkswagen Golf.
[2] 60 and 160 refer to number of kilometers vehicle can drive on fully charged battery.

so many factors are unpredictable. Governments could aggressively promote the use of electrified vehicles, for example, and then lose tax revenues when drivers spend less money on gasoline at the pump. Will lawmakers in Europe and the United States be willing to sacrifice tax receipts that pay for the upkeep of roads in order to help control climate change. If not, how will the tax burden be migrated to the new fuel: electricity? Besides, electrified vehicles are a nascent technology, and it's too early to say how the rate of adoption by consumers in different segments will evolve or how costs will be optimized.

But here's a number to contemplate: electrified vehicles would enter the mainstream if about 10 percent of all cars on the roads were battery-electric or plug-in vehicles, running solely on electric power. That would mean sales of six million to eight million electrified vehicles a year by 2020, which would change whole sectors dramatically. Let's look at the opportunities and challenges for the three key ones: autos, batteries, and utilities.

Automakers
Electrified vehicles pose an enormous threat to incumbent automakers. The internal-combustion engine and transmission are the core components they have focused on since outsourcing the manufacture of many other components and subassemblies. In a world where vehicles run on electrons rather than hydrocarbons, the automakers will have to reinvent their businesses to survive. Nonetheless, incumbency is also a strategic strength in this sector. Attackers face significant entry barriers, including manufacturing scale, brand equity, channel relationships (for instance, dealership networks), customer management, and capital.

Moreover, electrified vehicles open up opportunities for incumbent automakers. These cars could help them meet increasingly stringent emission regulations and avoid fines. The low-end torque of electric motors can accelerate cars more quickly, smoothly, and quietly, which could provide distinctive new value to buyers. Automakers could also beat attackers to the punch in tapping assets such as plants and dealership networks to introduce new business models, such as selling transport services rather than products. To achieve any of this, auto executives will need to consider the strategic role of electrified vehicles. The plans of the automakers, for example, must include a clear understanding of the way they will prioritize R&D across a portfolio of vehicle platforms, from hybrids to plug-in hybrids to battery-electric models to cars powered by internal-combustion engines.

Automakers should also consider how their relationships with the battery makers will evolve, as well as the role technology standards will play in fitting batteries into vehicles. (Most large automakers are currently partnering with battery companies to develop the electrified or hybrid vehicles they are preparing to launch.) Battery makers and tier-one suppliers will try to secure the value implicit in owning core skills, including innovation in batteries and in the new features they could make possible. Over time, value will probably shift from the battery cell to the electronics and software of the power- and thermal-management system, which determines a car's actual performance. Executives should develop plans to capture that value when the shift occurs.

Executives should consider the evolution of the downstream business too. Will utilities, gas stations, car companies, or other third parties own the recharging infrastructure and the real estate it occupies, for example? Will processing intelligence and data collection sit in the recharging infrastructure or in the vehicle? Strategists should also think about whether dealers or players like Wal-Mart will sell cars and batteries and about how the supply chain for electrified vehicles differs from the present one. In all likelihood, for instance, demand for lightweight materials will grow, while demand for exhaust systems and mufflers will shrink.

Battery producers

In a world where consumers buy six million to eight million electric-drive vehicles each year, annual sales of batteries might come to $60 billion, and value will start shifting to them from oil.[3] Over the long term, the sector's growth potential is vast, and even the near-term prospects look sunny. For now, battery makers can reap high margins from differentiated battery chemistries that provide a cost, performance, and safety edge. It also helps to win government grants, announced by the European Union and the United States as a stimulus measure to increase domestic battery capacity. The grants have been designed to attract additional private investment.

Nonetheless, battery manufacturers face many challenges. As capacity ramps up, the cells of batteries (their basic element)[4] will become a commodity, like many other automotive components. Value will migrate from the cell-level chemistry to the level of battery-pack systems, including power- and thermal-management software, and to the electronics optimizing a battery's performance in a specific vehicle. To retain value in the longer term, battery makers may want to partner more closely with the automakers' tier-one suppliers—which aggregate components into vehicle systems, such as steering systems or dashboards—or with the automakers themselves. The latter route would help battery makers preserve more value because they would supplant the tier-one suppliers, but to succeed they would have to obtain the

---

[3] Assuming 2020 battery pack costs of $350/kWh and a battery pack capacity of 14 kWh and 30 kWh for plug-in hybrid (60 km range) and battery-electric vehicle (160 km range), respectively.

[4] A typical battery used in automotive applications may contain 25 to 150 component cells, depending on the energy density of the battery and the cells.

required systems integration skills, knowledge of cars, and key auto relationships. Considering the resources needed to achieve these goals, battery makers would have to ask themselves whether they have the engineering resources to scale the necessary capabilities across a number of vehicle platforms, model derivatives, and OEMs.

Even in the near term, the battery makers can no longer put off some unresolved questions. How, for instance, will these companies protect their intellectual property in process-driven chemistries in order to prevent reverse engineering? One battery maker has spread different parts of its proprietary process across its factories in China, reducing the chance that former employees will reengineer the "secret recipe" for a competitor. So far, patents haven't been heavily contested, but that could change as volumes and revenues grow. This possibility, as well as the uncertain strength of key patents, means that battery companies must think carefully about how to defend their intellectual-property positions and whether to attack those of rivals. The most important question, however, may be which part of the value chain of batteries will take on the warranty risk associated with them. Car makers don't want to do so. Emerging battery companies may not have the balance sheets to offer warranties credibly. Incumbents with strong balance sheets and battery businesses—Johnson Controls, NEC, or Samsung, for instance—could provide this service if the opportunity looks ripe.

The evolution of the after-market for batteries is an open question. Since none of them have been tested in large numbers under the real (and diverse) driving conditions they will encounter over their lifetimes, it isn't clear yet how much residual value there will be. Indeed, batteries at the end of their lives may be liabilities, not assets, because of their recycling costs. (Ninety-seven percent of the lead in lead–acid batteries can be recycled, but lithium is trickier to handle and currently less valuable than lead.) Executives should bake the cost of managing lithium and other component materials into the business model or find ways to ensure that the cost accrues somewhere else in the value chain.

Leading battery makers are already thinking through ways to scale up manufacturing, because they know that there will be first-mover advantages, such as increased automation, increased procurement leverage, and new form factors. These companies are also investing significant sums in R&D for the next generation of battery chemistries. The reason is that the complicated interplay among a battery cell's core elements (such as the cathode, electrolyte, separator, and anode) determines different aspects of the cell's performance—for example, power density, energy density, safety, depth of charge, cycle life, and shelf life, which determine the choice of batteries for particular vehicles. Since cell materials account for 30 to 50 percent of the cost of a battery pack, many battery makers are also considering the pros and cons of integrating vertically into key materials.

Finally, battery makers should also think about the possibility of moving into new products or services. These might include offerings for transport sectors (such as maritime, locomotives, trucks, and buses) and for utilities, which might be interested in voltage and frequency regulation, power-management services, and bulk energy storage. Fast charging—applications to deliver lots of power to batteries very quickly, in minutes rather than hours—might be another source of revenues. All of these applications have very different energy and power density needs, as well as different capital requirements and operating expenses. Battery companies will need to place their bets and manage their portfolios carefully.

Utilities and infrastructure providers
Quite apart from electrified vehicles, policies to improve energy efficiency or reduce carbon emissions pose a serious challenge to utilities, whose revenues and profits will come under pressure as businesses, governments, and private homes—stimulated by government investments and by new standards and policies in China, Europe, and the United States—use energy more efficiently. Meanwhile, the utilities' per-unit generation costs will rise in the near term with the faster adoption of renewable forms of energy, such as solar and wind—intermittent sources that must be supported by a new transmission and distribution infrastructure. Furthermore, any carbon tax or cap-and-trade scheme will affect energy prices and, potentially, the utilities' long-term profitability.

Electrified vehicles, however, create new revenues for utilities. If 20 percent of the cars and trucks sold in a local market (for example, certain parts of California) over the next decade have electric drives, recharging them could represent up to 2 percent of total electricity demand, according to our analysis of local markets where electrified vehicles might take off first. If vehicles were charged mainly at night, utilities could satisfy much of this demand without installing any significant additional generation capacity.

The charging of electrified vehicles might help utilities profit from carbon-abatement taxes and trading mechanisms as well. These companies, for example, could take steps with their regulators to capture emission credit for the abatement that utilities make possible in the transport sector. In addition, they could reposition themselves in the minds of their customers not only as electricity companies but also as enablers of an environmentally sustainable economy. Any failure to play an active leadership role exposes utilities to the risk of being disintermediated in the residential or commercial segments by other service providers, such as large IT players that already have strong positions in homes (for instance, Cisco and IBM), or by emerging innovators.

Charging at night is the key, however. If utilities don't install smart systems that control the time when a vehicle can charge, they could struggle to meet peak demand, assuming, as many do, that owners will want to plug in their cars upon returning home in the evening. (Many utilities already struggle to provide enough power in the peak-use early-evening hours.) Worse, electrified-vehicle owners, especially in the early years, will probably cluster together in certain affluent neighborhoods. The incremental demand may be enough to blow out transformers in these areas and require new investments in power generation.

Blowouts would reduce the reliability of the system and the satisfaction of its customers, as well as require expensive investments. Electrified vehicles, we assume, will be twice as popular in certain markets in California than they will be in other parts of the United States. If sales of such vehicles reach 1.8 million in that state by 2020, inadequately managed charging could require upward of $5 billion in incremental investments in transmission and generation infrastructure. This incremental peak-time power will almost certainly come from fossil fuels, which will raise carbon dioxide emissions and force utilities to spend more for emission allowances if they can't get credit for the increased "well to wheel" efficiency of electrified vehicles.[5]

Related articles on mckinseyquarterly.com
An electric plan for energy resilience
What countries can do about cutting carbon emissions
Global roadmap for China's autos

To meet the challenge of charging vehicles and of a "smart" charging infrastructure, utilities must start planning now for the necessary technologies, costs, infrastructure partners, and business models. Regulated utilities could try to build the required investment into the rate base by convincing regulators of the business logic. They can also work with automakers to provide a seamless experience for consumers: when someone walks into a dealership to buy a new electrified car, the local utility should know—and be ready to install the right equipment in the customer's home.

The authors would like to thank Nadeem Sheikh for his substantial contributions to this article.

Copyright © 2009 McKinsey & Company. All rights reserved.

We welcome your comments on this article. Please send them to quarterly_comments@mckinsey.com.

Electrified vehicles will become a reality—sooner, as the bulls believe, or later, as the bears do. That will change the competitive landscape of the automotive, battery, and utilities sectors and have an impact on several others. Companies that act boldly and time their moves appropriately will probably enjoy significant gains; those that don't will not. But timing is critical: jumping in too early or late will be costly. Buckle up and hang on for the ride. o

[5] These emissions could be mitigated if new power facilities were located outside of cities and the emissions were captured and stored.

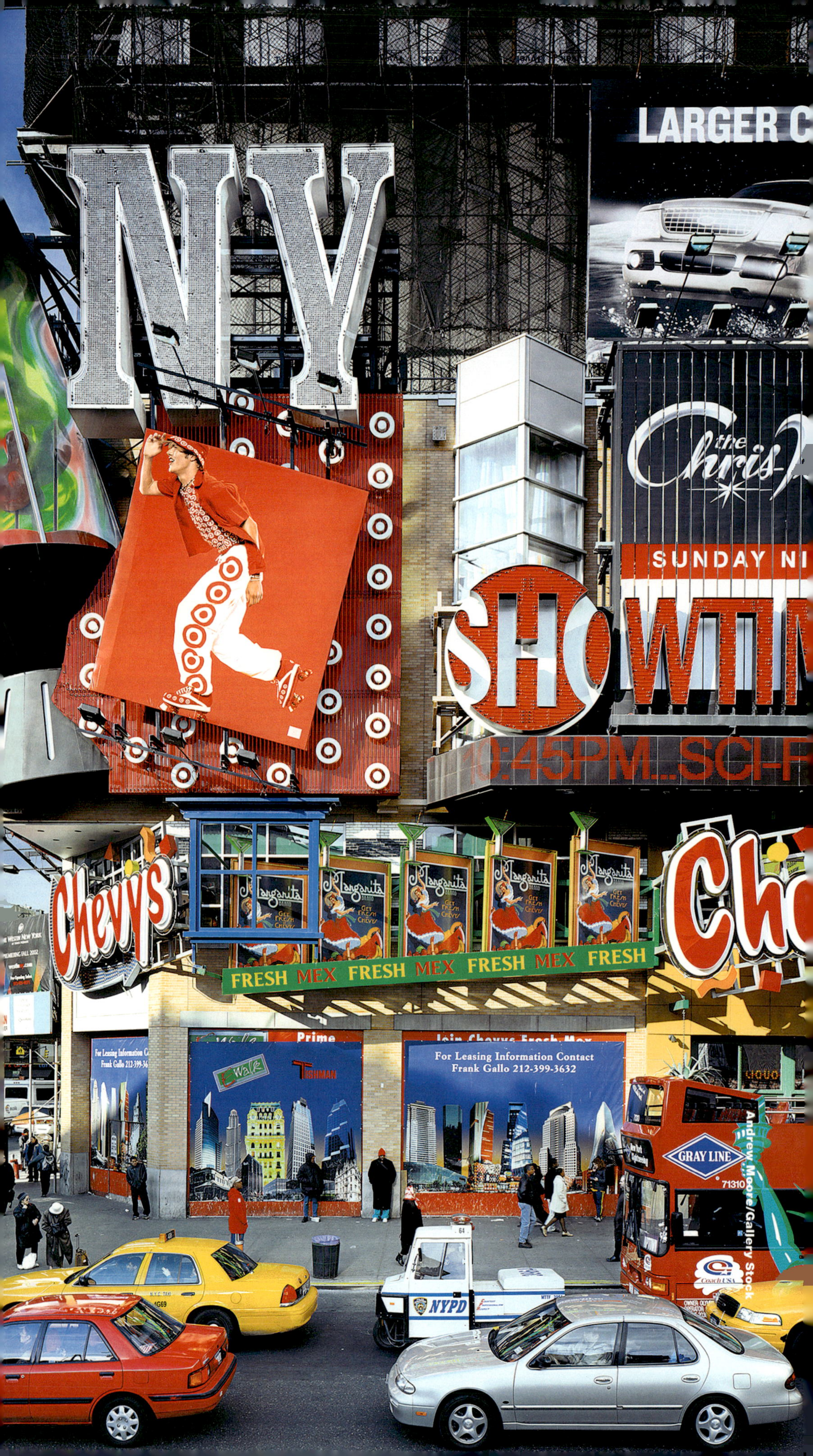

Andrew Moore/Gallery Stock

The consumer decision journey

Consumers are moving outside the purchasing funnel—changing the way they research and buy your products. If your marketing hasn't changed in response, it should.

David Court, Dave Elzinga, Susan Mulder, and Ole Jørgen Vetvik

If marketing has one goal, it's to reach consumers at the moments that most influence their decisions. That's why consumer electronics companies make sure not only that customers see their televisions in stores but also that those televisions display vivid high-definition pictures. It's why Amazon.com, a decade ago, began offering targeted product recommendations to consumers already logged in and ready to buy. And it explains P&G's decision, long ago, to produce radio and then TV programs to reach the audiences most likely to buy its products—hence, the term "soap opera."

Marketing has always sought those moments, or touch points, when consumers are open to influence. For years, touch points have been understood through the metaphor of a "funnel"—consumers start with a number of potential brands in mind (the wide end of the funnel), marketing is then directed at them as they methodically reduce that number and move through the funnel, and at the end they emerge with the one brand they chose to purchase (Exhibit 1). But today, the funnel concept fails to capture all the touch points and key buying factors resulting from the explosion of product choices and digital channels, coupled with the emergence of an increasingly discerning, well-informed consumer. A more sophisticated approach is required to help marketers navigate this environment, which is less linear

David Court is a director in McKinsey's Dallas office, Dave Elzinga is a principal in the Chicago office, Susie Mulder is a principal in the Boston office, and Ole Jørgen Vetvik is a principal in the Oslo office.

Exhibit 1

The traditional funnel

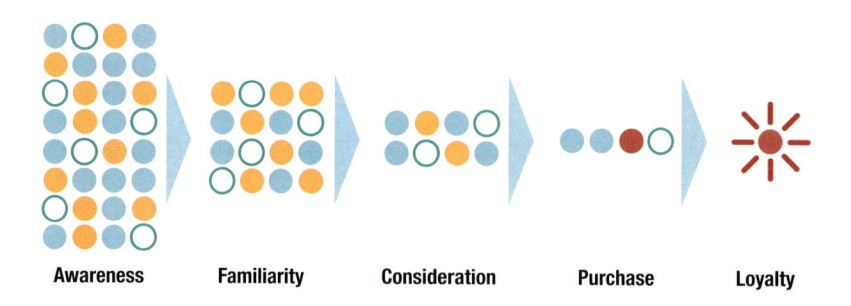

| Awareness | Familiarity | Consideration | Purchase | Loyalty |

and more complicated than the funnel suggests. We call this approach the *consumer decision journey*. Our thinking is applicable to any geographic market that has different kinds of media, Internet access, and wide product choice, including big cities in emerging markets such as China and India.

We developed this approach by examining the purchase decisions of almost 20,000 consumers across five industries and three continents. Our research showed that the proliferation of media and products requires marketers to find new ways to get their brands included in the initial-consideration set that consumers develop as they begin their decision journey. We also found that because of the shift away from one-way communication—from marketers to consumers— toward a two-way conversation, marketers need a more systematic way to satisfy customer demands and manage word-of-mouth. In addition, the research identified two different types of customer loyalty, challenging companies to reinvigorate their loyalty programs and the way they manage the customer experience.

An interactive exhibit explores the new consumer decision journey model and describes how marketers can use it to communicate with consumers at key stages in the decision-making process. Find the exhibit on mckinseyquarterly.com.

Finally, the research reinforced our belief in the importance not only of aligning all elements of marketing—strategy, spending, channel management, and message—with the journey that consumers undertake when they make purchasing decisions but also of integrating those elements across the organization. When marketers understand this journey and direct their spending and messaging to the moments of maximum influence, they stand a much greater chance of reaching consumers in the right place at the right time with the right message.

Exhibit 2

The consumer decision journey

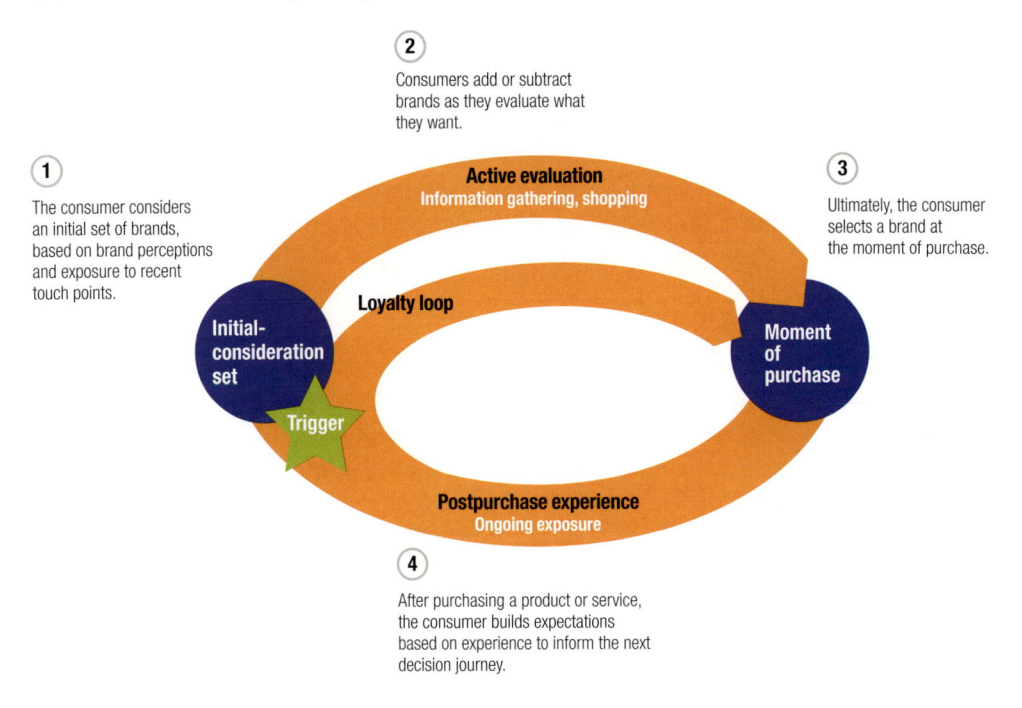

1 The consumer considers an initial set of brands, based on brand perceptions and exposure to recent touch points.

2 Consumers add or subtract brands as they evaluate what they want.

3 Ultimately, the consumer selects a brand at the moment of purchase.

4 After purchasing a product or service, the consumer builds expectations based on experience to inform the next decision journey.

- Active evaluation: Information gathering, shopping
- Loyalty loop
- Initial-consideration set
- Trigger
- Moment of purchase
- Postpurchase experience: Ongoing exposure

How consumers make decisions

Every day, people form impressions of brands from touch points such as advertisements, news reports, conversations with family and friends, and product experiences. Unless consumers are actively shopping, much of that exposure appears wasted. But what happens when something triggers the impulse to buy? Those accumulated impressions then become crucial because they shape the initial-consideration set: the small number of brands consumers regard at the outset as potential purchasing options.

The funnel analogy suggests that consumers systematically narrow the initial-consideration set as they weigh options, make decisions, and buy products. Then, the postsale phase becomes a trial period determining consumer loyalty to brands and the likelihood of buying their products again. Marketers have been taught to "push" marketing toward consumers at each stage of the funnel process to influence their behavior. But our qualitative and quantitative research in the automobile, skin care, insurance, consumer electronics, and mobile-telecom industries shows that something quite different now occurs.

Actually, the decision-making process is a more circular journey, with four primary phases representing potential battlegrounds where marketers can win or lose: initial consideration; active evaluation, or the process of researching potential purchases; closure, when consumers buy brands; and postpurchase, when consumers experience them (Exhibit 2). The funnel metaphor does help a good deal—for example, by providing a way to understand the strength of a brand compared with its competitors at different stages, highlighting the bottlenecks that stall adoption, and making it possible to focus on different aspects of the marketing challenge. Nonetheless, we found that in three areas profound changes in the way consumers make buying decisions called for a new approach.

Brand consideration

Imagine that a consumer has decided to buy a car. As with most kinds of products, the consumer will immediately be able to name an initial-consideration set of brands to purchase. In our qualitative research, consumers told us that the fragmenting of media and the proliferation of products have actually made them reduce the number of brands they consider at the outset. Faced with a plethora of choices and communications, consumers tend to fall back on the limited set of brands that have made it through the wilderness of messages. Brand awareness matters: brands in the initial-consideration set can be up to three times more likely to be purchased eventually than brands that aren't in it.

Not all is lost for brands excluded from this first stage, however. Contrary to the funnel metaphor, the number of brands under consideration during the active-evaluation phase may now actually expand rather than narrow as consumers seek information and

Exhibit 3

Adding brands

Sector	Share of purchases, %			Average number of brands	
	Initial consideration	Active evaluation	Loyalty loop[1]	In initial-consideration set	Added in active consideration
Autos	63	30	7	3.8	2.2
Personal computers	49	24	27	1.7	1.0
Skin care	38	37	25	1.5	1.8
Telecom carriers	38	20	42	1.5	0.9
Auto insurance	13	9	78	3.2	1.4

[1] For skin care, includes consumers who purchased their current brand 2 or more times in past 3 months and for whom current brand made up at least 70% of total category purchases in past 3 months; for all others, includes consumers who purchased same brand on current occasion as on previous occasion and did not consider any other brands.

Source: McKinsey consumer decision surveys: 2008 US auto and skin care, 2008 Germany mobile telecom, 2009 US auto insurance

shop a category. Brands may "interrupt" the decision-making process by entering into consideration and even force the exit of rivals. The number of brands added in later stages differs by industry: our research showed that people actively evaluating personal computers added an average of 1 brand to their initial-consideration set of 1.7, while automobile shoppers added 2.2 to their initial set of 3.8 (Exhibit 3). This change in behavior creates opportunities for marketers by adding touch points when brands can make an impact. Brands already under consideration can no longer take that status for granted.

Empowered consumers

The second profound change is that outreach of consumers to marketers has become dramatically more important than marketers' outreach to consumers. Marketing used to be driven by companies; "pushed" on consumers through traditional advertising, direct marketing, sponsorships, and other channels. At each point in the funnel, as consumers whittled down their brand options, marketers would attempt to sway their decisions. This imprecise approach often failed to reach the right consumers at the right time.

In today's decision journey, consumer-driven marketing is increasingly important as customers seize control of the process and actively "pull" information helpful to them. Our research found that two-thirds of the touch points during the active-evaluation phase involve consumer-driven marketing activities, such as Internet reviews and word-of-mouth recommendations from friends and family, as well as in-store interactions and recollections of past experiences. A third of the touch points involve company-driven marketing (Exhibit 4). Traditional marketing remains important, but the change in the way consumers make decisions means that marketers must move aggressively beyond purely push-style communication and learn to influence consumer-driven touch points, such as word-of-mouth and Internet information sites.

> Marketers must move aggressively beyond purely push-style communication and learn to influence consumer-driven touch points

The experience of US automobile manufacturers shows why marketers must master these new touch points. Companies like Chrysler and GM have long focused on using strong sales incentives and in-dealer programs to win during the active-evaluation and moment-of-purchase phases. These companies have been fighting the wrong battle: the real challenges for them are the initial-consideration and post-purchase phases, which Asian brands such as Toyota Motor and Honda

Exhibit 4

Where it counts

Most-influential touch points by stage of consumer decision journey, for competitors and new customers, % of effectiveness[1]

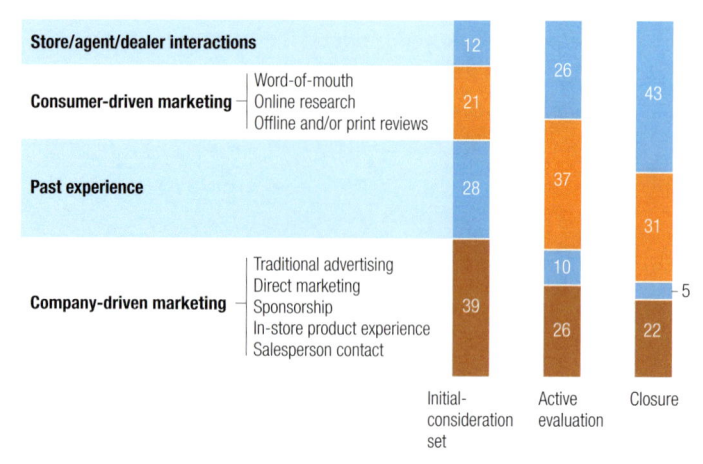

		Initial-consideration set	Active evaluation	Closure
Store/agent/dealer interactions		12	26	43
Consumer-driven marketing	Word-of-mouth / Online research / Offline and/or print reviews	21	37	31
Past experience		28	10	5
Company-driven marketing	Traditional advertising / Direct marketing / Sponsorship / In-store product experience / Salesperson contact	39	26	22

[1]Based on research conducted on German, Japanese, and US consumers in following sectors: for initial consideration—autos, auto insurance, telecom handsets and carriers; for active evaluation—auto insurance, telecom handsets; for closure—autos, auto insurance, skin care, and TVs; figures may not sum to 100%, because of rounding.

dominate with their brand strength and product quality. Positive experiences with Asian vehicles have made purchasers loyal to them, and that in turn generates positive word-of-mouth that increases the likelihood of their making it into the initial-consideration set. Not even constant sales incentives by US manufacturers can overcome this virtuous cycle.

Two types of loyalty

When consumers reach a decision at the moment of purchase, the marketer's work has just begun: the postpurchase experience shapes their opinion for every subsequent decision in the category, so the journey is an ongoing cycle. More than 60 percent of consumers of facial skin care products, for example, go online to conduct further research after the purchase—a touch point unimaginable when the funnel was conceived.

Although the need to provide an after-sales experience that inspires loyalty and therefore repeat purchases isn't new, not all loyalty is equal in today's increasingly competitive, complex world. Of consumers who profess loyalty to a brand, some are active loyalists, who not only stick with it but also recommend it. Others are passive loyalists who, whether from laziness or confusion caused by the dizzying array of choices, stay with a brand without being committed to it. Despite their claims of allegiance, passive consumers are open to messages from competitors that give them a reason to switch.

Take the automotive-insurance industry, in which most companies have a large base of seemingly loyal customers who renew every year. Our research found as much as a sixfold difference in the ratio of active to passive loyalists among major brands, so companies have opportunities to interrupt the loyalty loop. The US insurers GEICO and Progressive are doing just that, snaring the passively loyal customers of other companies by making comparison shopping and switching easy. They are giving consumers reasons to leave, not excuses to stay.

All marketers should make expanding the base of active loyalists a priority, and to do so they must focus their spending on the new touch points. That will require entirely new marketing efforts, not just investments in Internet sites and efforts to drive word-of-mouth or a renewed commitment to customer satisfaction.

Aligning marketing with the consumer decision journey
Developing a deep knowledge of how consumers make decisions is the first step. For most marketers, the difficult part is focusing strategies and spending on the most influential touch points. In some cases, the marketing effort's direction must change, perhaps from focusing brand advertising on the initial-consideration phase to developing Internet properties that help consumers gain a better understanding of the brand when they actively evaluate it. Other marketers may need to retool their loyalty programs by focusing on active rather than passive loyalists or to spend money on in-store activities or word-of-mouth programs. The increasing complexity of the consumer decision journey will force virtually all companies to adopt new ways of measuring consumer attitudes, brand performance, and the effectiveness of marketing expenditures across the whole process.

Without such a realignment of spending, marketers face two risks. First, they could waste money: at a time when revenue growth is critical and funding tight, advertising and other investments will be less effective because consumers aren't getting the right information at the right time. Second, marketers could seem out of touch—for instance, by trying to push products on customers rather than providing them with the information, support, and experience they want to reach decisions themselves.

Four kinds of activities can help marketers address the new realities of the consumer decision journey.

Prioritize objectives and spending
In the past, most marketers consciously chose to focus on either end of the marketing funnel—building awareness or generating loyalty among current customers. Our research reveals a need to be much

more specific about the touch points used to influence consumers as they move through initial consideration to active evaluation to closure. By looking just at the traditional marketing funnel's front or back end, companies could miss exciting opportunities not only to focus investments on the most important points of the decision journey but also to target the right customers.

In the skin care industry, for example, we found that some brands are much stronger in the initial-consideration phase than in active evaluation or closure. For them, our research suggests a need to shift focus from overall brand positioning—already powerful enough to ensure that they get considered—to efforts that make consumers act or to investments in packaging and in-store activities targeted at the moment of purchase.

Tailor messaging

For some companies, new messaging is required to win in whatever part of the consumer journey offers the greatest revenue opportunity. A general message cutting across all stages may have to be replaced by one addressing weaknesses at a specific point, such as initial consideration or active evaluation.

Take the automotive industry. A number of brands in it could grow if consumers took them into consideration. Hyundai, the South Korean car manufacturer, tackled precisely this problem by adopting a marketing campaign built around protecting consumers financially by allowing them to return their vehicles if they lose their jobs. This provocative message, tied to something very real for Americans, became a major factor in helping Hyundai break into the initial-consideration set of many new consumers. In a poor automotive market, the company's market share is growing.

> Broadband connectivity lets marketers provide rich applications to consumers learning about products

Invest in consumer-driven marketing

To look beyond funnel-inspired push marketing, companies must invest in vehicles that let marketers interact with consumers as they learn about brands. The epicenter of consumer-driven marketing is the Internet, crucial during the active-evaluation phase as consumers seek information, reviews, and recommendations. Strong performance at this point in the decision journey requires a mind-set shift from buying media to developing properties that attract consumers: digital assets such as Web sites about products, programs to foster word-of-mouth, and systems that customize advertising by viewing the context and the consumer. Many organizations face the difficult and, at times, risky venture of shifting money to fundamentally new properties, much as P&G invested to gain radio exposure in the 1930s and television exposure in the 1950s.

Broadband connectivity, for example, lets marketers provide rich applications to consumers learning about products. Simple, dynamic tools that help consumers decide which products make sense for them are now essential elements of an online arsenal. American Express's card finder and Ford's car configurator, for example, rapidly and visually sort options with each click, making life easier for consumers at every stage of the decision journey. Marketers can influence online word-of-mouth by using tools that spot online conversations about brands, analyze what's being said, and allow marketers to post their own comments.

Finally, content-management systems and online targeting engines let marketers create hundreds of variations on an advertisement, taking into account the context where it appears, the past behavior of viewers, and a real-time inventory of what an organization needs to promote. For instance, many airlines manage and relentlessly optimize thousands of combinations of offers, prices, creative content, and formats to ensure that potential travelers see the most relevant opportunities. Digital marketing has long promised this kind of targeting. Now we finally have the tools to make it more accurate and to manage it cost effectively.

Win the in-store battle

Our research found that one consequence of the new world of marketing complexity is that more consumers hold off their final purchase decision until they're in a store. Merchandising and packaging have therefore become very important selling factors, a point that's not widely understood. Consumers want to look at a product in action and are highly influenced by the visual dimension: up to 40 percent of them change their minds because of something they see, learn, or do at this point—say, packaging, placement, or interactions with salespeople.

In skin care, for example, some brands that are fairly unlikely to be in a consumer's initial-consideration set nonetheless win at the point of purchase with attractive packages and on-shelf messaging. Such elements have now become essential selling tools because consumers of these products are still in play when they enter a store. That's also true in some consumer electronics segments, which explains those impressive rows of high-definition TVs in stores.

Sometimes it takes a combination of approaches—great packaging, a favorable shelf position, forceful fixtures, informative signage—to attract consumers who enter a store with a strong attachment to their initial-consideration set. Our research shows that in-store touch points provide a significant opportunity for other brands.

Integrating all customer-facing activities

In many companies, different parts of the organization undertake specific customer-facing activities—including informational Web sites, PR, and loyalty programs. Funding is opaque. A number of executives are responsible for each element, and they don't coordinate their work or even communicate. These activities must be integrated and given appropriate leadership.

The necessary changes are profound. A comprehensive view of all customer-facing activities is as important for business unit heads as for CEOs and chief marketing officers. But the full scope of the consumer decision journey goes beyond the traditional role of CMOs, who in many companies focus on brand building, advertisements, and perhaps market research. These responsibilities aren't going away. What's now required of CMOs is a broader role that realigns marketing with the current realities of consumer decision making, intensifies efforts to shape the public profiles of companies, and builds new marketing capabilities.

Related articles on mckinseyquarterly.com
The downturn's new rules for marketers
Profiting from proliferation
The evolving role of the CMO

Consider the range of skills needed to manage the customer experience in the automotive-insurance industry, in which some companies have many passive loyalists who can be pried away by rivals. Increasing the percentage of active loyalists requires not only integrating customer-facing activities into the marketing organization but also more subtle forms of organizational cooperation. These include identifying active loyalists through customer research, as well as understanding what drives that loyalty and how to harness it with word-of-mouth programs. Companies need an integrated, organization-wide "voice of the customer," with skills from advertising to public relations, product development, market research, and data management. It's hard but necessary to unify these activities, and the CMO is the natural candidate to do so.

• • •

Marketers have long been aware of profound changes in the way consumers research and buy products. Yet a failure to change the focus of marketing to match that evolution has undermined the core goal of reaching customers at the moments that most influence their purchases. The shift in consumer decision making means that marketers need to adjust their spending and to view the change not as a loss of power over consumers but as an opportunity to be in the right place at the right time, giving them the information and support they need to make the right decisions. o

The authors wish to acknowledge the contributions of Mary Ellen Coe, Jonathan Doogan, Ewan Duncan, Betsy Holden, and Brian Salsberg.

Copyright © 2009 McKinsey & Company. All rights reserved.

We welcome your comments on this article. Please send them to quarterly_comments@mckinsey.com.

The crisis:
Planning for uncertainty

109
M&A in a downturn:
Timing strategic moves

115
Just-in-time budgeting for a volatile economy

122
Strategic planning in a crisis

Artwork by Daniel Chang

M&A in a downturn:
Timing strategic moves

Timing is key as companies weigh whether to make strategic investments now or wait for clear signs of recovery. Scenario analysis can expose the risks of moving too quickly or slowly.

Richard Dobbs and Timothy M. Koller

Richard Dobbs is a director in McKinsey's Seoul office, and **Tim Koller** is a principal in the New York office.

It may be a nice problem to have, but even companies with healthy finances face a quandary: should they pursue acquisitions and invest in new projects now or wait for clear signs of a lasting recovery? On the one hand, the growing range of attractive—even once-in-a-lifetime— acquisitions and other investment opportunities not only seems hard to pass up but also includes some that weren't possible just a few years ago. Back then, buyers faced competition from private-equity firms flush with cash, governments applied antitrust regulations more strictly, and owners were less willing to sell. What's more, investments in capital projects, R&D, talent, or marketing are now tantalizingly cheaper than they have been, on average, over the economic cycle. On the other hand, many indicators suggest that the economy has yet to hit bottom. Companies that move too soon risk catching the proverbial falling knife, in the form of share prices that continue to plummet, or spending the cash they'll need to weather a long downturn.

Timing such moves is bound to be difficult. How quickly the world economy returns to normal—and indeed, what "normal" is going to be—will depend on hard-to-predict factors such as the fluctuations of consumer and business confidence, the actions of governments, and the volatility of global capital markets. Identifying market troughs will be particularly hard because stock indexes can rally and decline several times before the general direction becomes clear. In previous recessions, as many as six rallies were followed by market declines before the eventual troughs were reached.[1] During the current downturn, market indexes fluctuated by an average of 20 percent each month from November 2008 to March 2009.

Given the uncertainty, executives may easily give up in frustration, hunker down, and await irrefutable evidence that the economy is turning around. But this approach could be a recklessly cautious one. Instead, executives must make educated decisions now by weighing the risks of waiting or of moving too early. And while better timing of acquisitions, and therefore the prices paid for them, can make a big difference in their ability to create value, the best way to minimize risk is to ensure that investments have a strong strategic rationale.

Executives considering whether to jump back into M&A or to make other strategic investments now must understand what lies behind earnings and valuations. To illustrate the risks, we conducted an analysis of a hypothetical acquisition. Real US market and economic data allowed us to build a range of scenarios embodying different assumptions about future US economic performance.[2] We found that even scenarios assuming conservative levels of market performance (as indicated by the experience of past recessions) suggest that many industries may be reaching the point when acting sooner would be as appropriate as—if not better than—acting later. Managers who wait may be failing to maximize the creation of value.

Analyzing scenarios

The primary drivers of capital markets are levels of long-term profits and growth, so we define our scenarios in those terms. Long-term profits are tightly linked to the economy's overall performance: over the past 40 years, they have fluctuated around a stable 5 percent of GDP[3] (Exhibit 1). It's therefore reasonable to assume that a return to normal for corporate profits would mean a return to their long-term level relative to GDP and that long-term growth in corporate earnings will also be in line with long-term GDP. For our scenarios, we assume that US corporate profits will revert to some 5 percent of

---

[1] As of the end of March 2009, the present downturn had seen five so-called bear market rallies. This downturn could be different from past ones, so there could be more than the earlier maximum of six such rallies. As of March 2009, the market was about 18 months past its peak. The time to trough was 32 months in the 2000 recession, 21 months in the recession of the 1980s, 21 months in the recession of the 1970s, and 35 months in the Great Depression.
[2] Managers using this approach for actual strategic decisions would need to refine it by country, economic sector, or both, or to reflect the peculiarities of investments such as capital, R&D, or marketing expenditures, as well as competitors' moves and regulators' changes.
[3] We've excluded financial institutions from this analysis because their recent profits have been highly volatile—way above average in 2005–06 and way below average in 2007–08. The inclusion of these companies would not change the results but would make it harder to interpret the long-term trends.

Exhibit 1

Profits revert to the mean

Ratio of nonfinancial corporate profits to GDP,[1] %

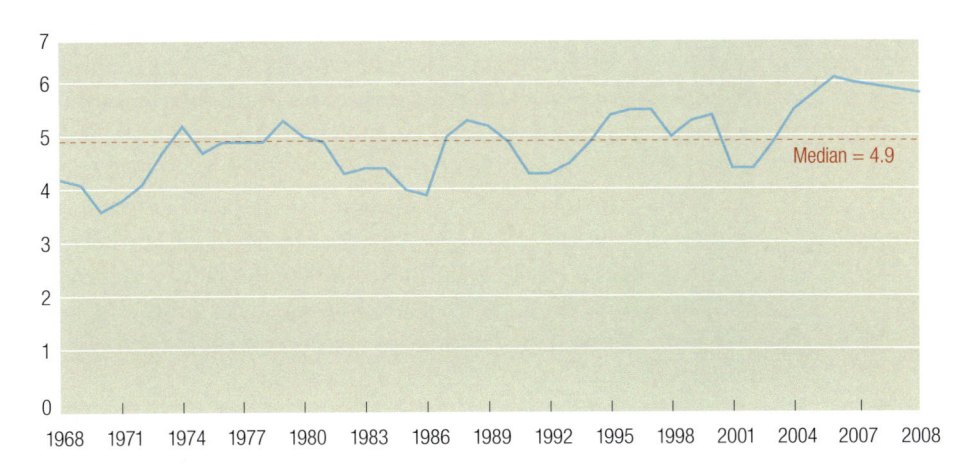

Median = 4.9

1968 1971 1974 1977 1980 1983 1986 1989 1992 1995 1998 2001 2004 2007 2008

[1]Includes all US-based nonfinancial companies with real revenues greater than $100 million. Profits are earnings before interest, taxes, and amortization (EBITA), less estimated taxes.

US GDP, although that estimate could be a conservative one if the trend to higher profits in the years leading up to the crisis resulted from a structural change in the economy. One can tailor this analysis to the circumstances of individual industries by developing a more detailed understanding of the linkages among GDP, revenue, and earnings.

Growth in the labor force and productivity drive the long-term growth of real GDP. Since it has historically grown in the range of 2.5 to 3.0 percent a year and returned to its former trend line in all US downturns from the Great Depression onward, with no permanent loss in GDP once the economy recovered, our base scenario assumes that both of those trends will continue. (We also examined scenarios reflecting the possibility that long-term GDP growth might be lower as a result of changing demographics, declining productivity growth, and the effects of the current financial crisis or that GDP might fall permanently by as much as 5 or 10 percent.) Finally, in normal conditions the market as a whole has a price-to-earnings ratio ranging from 15 to 17. We used that multiple in our 2.5–3.0 percent growth scenario and a lower one (14 to 16) in our 2.0–2.5 percent growth scenario. Both multiples are consistent with a discounted cash flow valuation of companies.[4]

[4]For more on our model of market valuation, see Marc H. Goedhart, Bin Jiang, and Timothy Koller, "The irrational component of your stock price," mckinseyquarterly.com, July 2006.

Under the scenario that most resembles the course of previous recessions (no permanent loss of GDP and 2.5 to 3.0 percent long-term real growth), the stock market's normal value in early 2009 (as measured by the S&P 500) would have been about 1,200 to 1,350. This implies that the stock market was trading, as of the end of March, at a discount of about 30 to 40 percent from its normal value (Exhibit 2). The discount is much lower under the more negative scenarios, but even in the worst of them—an unprecedented 10 percent decline and a limited recovery—the market is still valued at a small discount. You would have to expect a permanent GDP reduction of around 20 percent to see the March S&P 500 index level (around 800) as normal. A similar analysis for the performance of the stock market in previous recessions finds that at the trough of deeper recessions, it typically trades at a discount greater than 30 percent from its normal value (Exhibit 3).

Current stock prices can be interpreted in several ways. Perhaps the market is experiencing levels of pessimism typical of previous

Exhibit 2

Estimating stock market value

Scenario, %		Normal level, S&P 500 index equivalent	Market discount, from normal level, %
Assuming this level of permanent GDP loss . . .	. . . plus this level of long-term real growth		
0	2.5–3.0	1,200–1,350	30–40
0	2.0–2.5	1,100–1,250	25–35
5	2.5–3.0	1,100–1,250	25–35
5	2.0–2.5	1,050–1,200	20–30
10	2.0–2.5	1,000–1,150	15–25

Exhibit 3

Discounts in earlier recessions

Discount from stock market trough to normal value, %

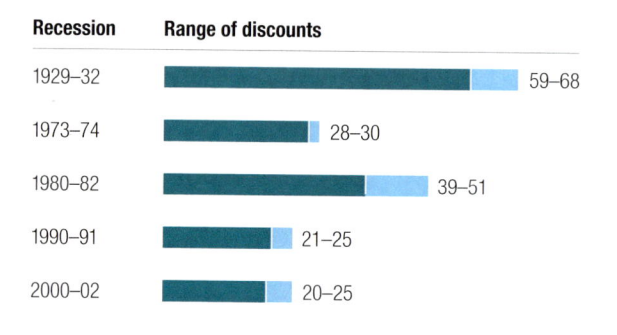

Recession	Range of discounts
1929–32	59–68
1973–74	28–30
1980–82	39–51
1990–91	21–25
2000–02	20–25

downturns, with the same opportunities for investors and acquirers. Or it may assign a reasonably high probability to a large, permanent GDP decline, which can't be ruled out even though it didn't happen in past downturns since, and including, the Great Depression. Finally, given the different nature of this downturn, the old relationships among GDP, profits, and stock prices may no longer hold, or in the future investors will demand higher returns from the market.

Timing the recovery

Strong companies deciding whether to move forward now with acquisitions or major capital projects should weigh further data on the timing of a stock market recovery. One common analysis calculates how many years must pass before the market will return to normal, assuming growth at the historical long-term average rate (10 percent a year). In past recessions, however, the stock market returned from the trough much more quickly, with cumulative returns, over the two years that followed it, of 50 percent to 130 percent (Exhibit 4).[5] If this pattern holds in the current downturn, there's a real danger that companies waiting too long will miss the upside of the rebound.

Such an analysis of earnings and stock markets can help companies evaluate the pros and cons of waiting or acting now. Assume, for ease of analysis, just two scenarios: either the market is currently at its trough, or it will decline by an additional 20 percent, reaching its trough in six months, so that the S&P 500 falls from its current level to around 640. A company attempting to time the market for a planned acquisition could make its move at any point, but let's assume three: it invests now, in six months, or in a year. For the purposes of our analysis, we assume that the market and the economy will return to normal in three years under either scenario, though clearly these are not the only possibilities.

[5] This analysis looks at share prices relative to the trough. Much more time may elapse before the market reaches the prior peak, partly because it wasn't based on fundamentals.

Exhibit 4

Speedy recovery

Recession	Pace of recovery, cumulative total returns to shareholders (TRS), %		
	1 year	2 years	3 years
1929–32	129	123	176
1973–74	46	85	79
1980–82	66	79	113
1990–91	34	48	72
2000–02	36	50	63

Exhibit 5

Now, or later?

Net present value (NPV) of alternative investment decisions

	Invest now	Invest in 6 months	Invest in 12 months
Market at trough now	100	55	38
Market declines by further 20% over next 6 months	100	122	104

In this simplified example, only timing an investment perfectly, in six months under scenario two, would produce a net present value (NPV) meaningfully better than the one resulting from investing now (Exhibit 5). If a company didn't hit the timing precisely, it could easily end up with a much lower NPV. This type of approach can also establish what you'd have to believe for "wait and see" to be the right strategy, but the analysis must be tailored to a specific industry or country and to the type of investment, such as M&A, capital expenditures, R&D, or marketing. The approach can also be tailored to analyze other risks, such as the possibility that competitors could preempt strategic moves, that regulators could become less accommodating, that companies could run out of capital, or that other, more favorable, investment opportunities might become available should the downturn deepen.

Much uncertainty surrounds the timing of the downturn's end, but companies waiting for clear evidence of a turnaround may find that they have been recklessly cautious and missed once-in-a-generation opportunities to acquire or invest. Executives considering when to make their next strategic moves can learn much by examining the course of previous downturns—particularly how valuation levels were related to corporate earnings and how valuations and earnings were related to the economy as a whole.

Related articles on mckinseyquarterly.com
What's different about M&A in this downturn
Learning to love recessions
Financial crises, past and present

The authors would like to thank Bing Cao, Ezra Greenberg, John Horn, and Bin Jiang for their contributions to this article.

Copyright © 2009 McKinsey & Company. All rights reserved.

We welcome your comments on this article. Please send them to quarterly_comments@mckinsey.com.

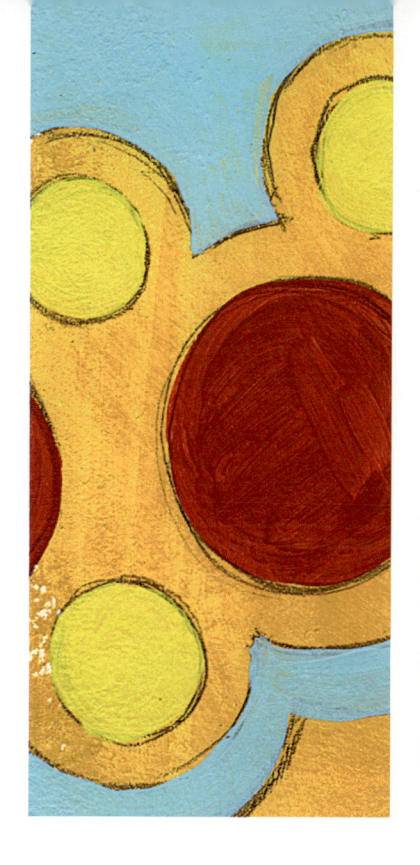

Just-in-time budgeting for a volatile economy

A volatile economy makes traditional budgets obsolete before they're even completed. Here's how companies can adapt more quickly.

Mahmut Akten, Massimo Giordano, and Mari A. Scheiffele

Most companies find budgeting a formidable challenge even under stable conditions. Managers often spend significant amounts of time on it, only to be dismayed by how little value comes from four to six months' effort. Under volatile conditions, when economic forecasts change from week to week, developing one reliable budget to coordinate business units and track performance for an entire fiscal year is very difficult. Following the traditional budget process may even be unproductive.

There's no easy fix, particularly for very large corporations, and companies that have tried to solve the problem don't have much of a track record. Executives can, however, take several measures to make the process more effective: for instance, scenario planning, zero-based budgeting, rolling forecasts, and quarterly budgeting. Central to all of them is a substantial increase in the CFO's role and a radical speeding up of the budgeting process.

Mahmut Akten is a consultant in McKinsey's Istanbul office, **Massimo Giordano** is a director in the Milan office, and **Mari Scheiffele** is a principal in the Zurich office.

New approaches

For many companies, allocating or withholding resources quickly and efficiently may be the only way to navigate today's very tough environment. A completely new approach to the budget process is often needed. The list that follows isn't exhaustive, nor are the activities on it mutually exclusive. In some combination—depending on the business, size, complexity, and culture of the organization involved—they can help companies improve the budget process.

1. Scenario planning with trigger events

In more stable times, the budget process is typically an exercise in consensus building—a lengthy and difficult effort to generate a single view of the future to guide a company's investments and rewards over the coming year. While many management teams speculate informally on how their businesses will evolve, few actively debate a number of scenarios or undertake the concrete short- and long-term financial analyses that would make such a debate meaningful. The process therefore isn't agile enough to respond to sudden, dramatic changes in the economy. Any revisions to the budget as the year unfolds are reactive and backward focused rather than reflecting an informed view of alternative future scenarios.

Executives at some forward-thinking companies, however, have not only formally developed concrete macroeconomic and business scenarios, including some considered extreme,[1] but also modeled the implications of each scenario for their own businesses and customers, as well as for competitors. At the end of the process, these companies adopted a single budget, but they supplemented it with concrete alternative financial statements and business plans based on plausible future scenarios. This approach lets companies build flexibility into their cost structures—for instance, through the outsourcing of services or the use of contingent purchasing contracts—so they can more easily shift from the primary budget if necessary.

Furthermore, these companies have also identified the handful of events—say, a change in the availability of short-term funding, the bankruptcy of major customers or suppliers, or a specific market share decline—that would trigger a shift from the primary scenario to an alternative. CFOs and the finance function monitor these trigger points and stand ready to alert the executive team if risk levels breach well-defined thresholds. The entire executive team would then immediately implement the predetermined contingency plans.

At one global health care products company, for example, executives monitor sales of specific premium product lines, a key indicator of the future course of revenues and profitability. When the executives saw that customers were buying fewer premium products and greater numbers of basic ones—or none at all—they shifted to a different

---

[1] See Richard Dobbs, Massimo Giordano, and Felix Wenger, "The CFO's role in navigating the downturn," mckinseyquarterly.com, February 2009.

budget and withheld part of the company's planned second-half 2009 spending until the first-quarter numbers were clear. This company is actually growing and doing quite well, but when its trigger points suggested weakness in a key indicator, executives quickly adapted their approach to resources and investments for the rest of the year.

It's important to note that the CFO need not apply contingency plans to the whole organization; changes can be limited to specific business units, while others continue to implement the current budget. Managers of the affected units must then develop and apply new budgets and incentives and reconsider hedging strategies, capital allocations, and funding.

2. Zero-based budgeting

Amid today's extreme uncertainty, most companies are cutting discretionary expenditures. The typical budget process is not, however, designed to make managers rethink their business models if the recession persists or shifts the economy in a fundamental way. On the contrary, many current budgets are anchored in past ones, with incremental changes to adjust for inflation or specific product trends.

Zero-based budgeting was developed during the inflationary environment of the mid-1970s to avoid precisely this trap.[2] It starts the process wholly from scratch, assuming different end points for different industries and businesses, such as a 30 percent smaller overall market or a modified organization or portfolio. Operating and capital expenditures are then prioritized according to their alignment with the company's strategy and their expected returns on investment. Breaking down the budget into such discrete funding decisions makes it easier for the CFO and other senior executives to choose among competing claims on scarce resources.

Consider, for example the telecom industry, which has changed significantly in the past decade. Most incumbent operators project lower revenues in the near future but must still invest significantly in next-generation networks to be viable in the long term. To balance these competing demands, a European telecom player recently started a zero-based budgeting process by disaggregating its expenditures into logical decision units addressing different types of expenses, such as new capital expenditures (say, building a third-generation network) or maintenance. Each decision unit's capital expenditures (such as those for meeting license requirements or growth in a targeted city) were then classified as "keep," "discuss," or "cut." Finally, executives based the priority of each capital expenditure on its financial returns

---

[2] Zero-based budgeting, first named by Peter Pyhrr in the *Harvard Business Review* (1970), gained prominence during the 1970s, particularly when President Carter introduced zero-based budgeting into the federal budget process, in 1977. See Peter A. Pyhrr, "Zero-base budgeting," *Harvard Business Review*, 1970, Volume 48, Number 6, pp. 111–21.

and alignment with the company's strategy. After only a few iterations, the company reached its target capital expenditure level—a 20 percent reduction, which nonetheless supported investment in future growth.

Clearly, this approach can add a couple of months to an already long process. We therefore recommend zero-based budgeting only for areas promising the highest potential savings—for instance, capital expenditures, certain operating expenditures, and very focused costs, such as procurement. It's useful to identify a company's biggest expenses and which of them can realistically be cut. Some costs, such as those for employees or a branch network's real estate, are relatively inflexible and hard to change. Others, such as advertising or most capital expenditures, could be reset from scratch every year.

3. Rolling forecasts

Most companies prepare informal earnings forecasts on a monthly or quarterly basis, usually in a planning group within the finance department. These forecasts, seldom tied to active decisions about the budget's management, almost always involve nothing more than updated projections of year-end values. As a result, the company-wide process is opaque, no one is accountable for the outcome, and projections for the rest of the year are less and less valuable as it progresses. At one global Internet provider, this haphazard approach meant that some business units projected meeting their full-year earnings targets despite growing gaps between the forecasts and the actual numbers. The finance department, trying to explain the actual numbers and to propose ways of closing the gaps, found itself caught between the CEO and the chief operating officer (COO) on the one hand and the heads of business units on the other. By the time the business units acknowledged that they would miss their targets, it was too late to take compensatory action.

Some leading companies have formalized a process that involves rolling 12- to 18-month forecasts for the most important financial variables. This approach increases the visibility of the process and accountability for it so that CFOs can act when forecasts start to diverge from actual performance. In companies we've observed, the CFO manages the process, convening business leaders, the CEO, and the COO each month or quarter to identify gaps and discuss how to close them. Typically, a good, hard debate among business units examines their performance and generates a way forward.

For companies that aren't accustomed to this kind of collaboration on their budgets, it represents a big cultural change: managers are accountable for their promises and must collectively adapt to the fast-changing macroeconomic climate. At the global Internet provider, simply getting everyone into the same room to discuss the growing gaps between forecasts and performance was a challenge. The CFO had to orchestrate a mind-set shift so that the managers of different units rallied around one another to solve the problem.

4. Quarterly budgeting

In periods of extreme uncertainty, some companies may need to set aside their long-term goals and concentrate on the next three months. Companies under that much stress, especially those attempting a turn around, ought to abandon annual budgeting and switch to a more tactical quarter-by-quarter process. These companies should focus on cutting costs and on managing their working capital and short-term financial needs, not on developing annual revenue or profit guidance. The quarterly approach allows companies to allocate their resources in real time, to make better forecasts, and to review their performance at the end of each quarter and therefore identify and address problems more quickly.

In the longer run, quarter-by-quarter budgeting can stunt growth by overemphasizing the short term. CFOs and their companies should return to focusing on the long term, with annual budgets, as soon as possible.

General improvements

Whether a company sticks to its traditional approach, implements one of the new ones described above, or combines them to meet its own needs, it should also improve the budgeting process as a whole. These improvements take time to implement, but when carried out from the top down, by the CFO and other senior executives, they can limit the amount of cumbersome work an organization must undertake at the end of each quarter.

Key metrics

At a time when priorities and, indeed, the very business environment itself are changing rapidly, companies must review their key performance indicators (KPIs). Today's focus on cash and risk management requires a reevaluation of metrics relevant to the quality, liquidity, and returns of assets and a shift away from the revenue and growth indicators emphasized in recent years. Often, the new focus just means reprioritizing performance metrics when budgets are prepared or incentive systems linked. Executives must also constantly assess the quality and health of all performance cells[3] in order to

[3] For a perspective on how to reorganize performance cells by implementing a value creation approach, see Massimo Giordano and Felix Wenger, "Organizing for value," mckinseyquarterly.com, July 2008.

detect any deterioration in key metrics—such as the number of orders or customers or the churn rate—more quickly.

A shorter process
The time the budget process consumes must fall dramatically: it can no longer start in September and go on until February or March, as it does at many companies. They can speed up the pace sufficiently only by substantially increasing the amount of top-down guidance from the CFO, synthesizing tracked KPIs, and eliminating formal bureaucracy. In the usual approach, for example, top management introduces a budget that descends to the front line for fleshing out in detail and then returns to the top for finalizing. One way CFOs could accelerate the process would be to conduct negotiations between top managers and the divisions during the first iteration and leave the divisions to manage the budget's implementation by the front line.

Level of detail
If an existing budget needs updating rather than rewriting, a company doesn't have to update it at the original level of detail. Business unit managers in many companies imagine that deep specifics and full financial statements reflect greater accuracy. At the level of individual units, for any given year, it's hard to disprove that idea. Many business unit leaders produce a conservative budget, however, so that they are sure to meet or exceed expectations at the year's end. When such unit-level numbers are aggregated, the resulting company-wide numbers are wildly off the mark. Knowing that business unit managers are typically too conservative, executives may pad their forecasts, making the end product all the more unreliable. On occasion, however, individual business units are too aggressive, and that's why one global construction company, for example, missed its aggregate production targets for more than a decade. Less data can actually be more meaningful data if executives restrict the projections of business units to top-line estimates.

Related articles on mckinseyquarterly.com
What next? Ten questions for CFOs
The CFO's role in navigating the downturn
Toward a leaner finance department

Incentives
Any time a budget is modified, changes to forecasts and expectations can affect management's compensation levels and bonuses. Such incentives are typically aligned with specific levels of budget line items, such as volume forecasts, that companies may have to change so they can adapt to volatile economic conditions. Those conditions can

render bonuses null as a performance incentive anyway. Why strive to meet a volume target, for example, if the downturn makes it unlikely that you will?

Updating incentives when budgets change appeals to some people but may create great complexity in practice. Negotiating new targets and resetting incentives can politicize the budget process as managers maneuver to impose their own mind-sets: lowering targets to beat them comfortably. New targets and incentives also distract attention from the need to review the business plan and the allocation of resources.

A more appropriate way of structuring incentives is to start using relative targets—such as market share, cost metrics, or health indicators (say, customer satisfaction)—excluding uncontrollable variables. Such targets (for instance, the cost of an airline seat exclusive of expenses for fuel) are relatively insensitive to macro-conditions and thus motivate managers to build the business no matter which scenario comes to pass.

• • •

These times of economic volatility call for a faster budget process more closely connected to strategy through the CFO's active intervention. Despite the special challenges, companies can greatly improve their chances of coping with the uncertainty they now confront.

Copyright © 2009 McKinsey & Company. All rights reserved.

We welcome your comments on this article. Please send them to quarterly_comments@mckinsey.com.

Strategic planning in a crisis

Commentary from McKinsey experts and *Quarterly* readers

Andrew Cheung, Eric Kutcher, and Dilip Wagle

Strategists, now facing the most profoundly uncertain times in their careers, are creating disaster scenarios that would have been unthinkable until recently and making the preservation of cash integral to their strategies. These are uncharted waters, and no one has a clear map for sailing through them.

This spring, when companies were in the midst of their planning, we posted an article, "Strategic planning: Three tips for 2009,"[1] on our Web site offering three suggestions based on our recent experience in strategic planning. The first is considering more variables and involving more decision makers than they have in the past. Second, strategists need to place a greater emphasis on monitoring to recognize when changing conditions merit quick strategic adjustments. Third, they must look beyond the crisis. A focus on new or surprising scenarios shouldn't obscure relevant long-term trends or devalue important existing strategies.

But in this fast-moving environment, no one has all the answers. So we invited readers to share their recent experiences first through an online survey and then in a more open-ended online discussion. Taken together, these ideas provide helpful food for thought for strategists.

Andrew Cheung is an associate principal in McKinsey's Silicon Valley office, **Eric Kutcher** is a principal in the Stamford office, and **Dilip Wagle** is a principal in the Seattle office.

[1] See Renée Dye, Olivier Sibony, and S. Patrick Viguerie, "Strategic planning: Three tips for 2009," mckinseyquarterly.com, April 2009.

Survey results

The survey results indicate that many strategists seem to be rapidly adjusting their planning processes to cope with the changed economic environment. The changes executives say have been most significant are the adoption of a more rigorous approach to approving projects and capital spending—presumably with an eye toward managing cash carefully—and the creation of strategies that are more dynamic, focus on the short term, and that include more analyses (exhibit).

Scenario planning is becoming a leading part of the process: more than 50 percent of respondents say it is either playing a bigger role in their companies' strategic planning this year or has been newly added to the process. Further, nearly 60 percent of the respondents say their companies are monitoring progress against their strategic planning more frequently this year. More than 80 percent are assessing the progress of their strategic plans at least quarterly, with 50 percent doing so at least once a month.

One red flag: more than 50 percent express worry about not striking the right balance between near-term challenges and long-term strategic priorities.

Exhibit

Most significant changes in company's strategic-planning process, % of respondents

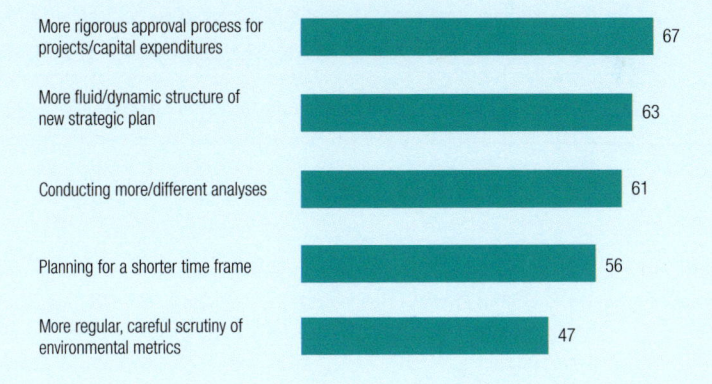

Change	%
More rigorous approval process for projects/capital expenditures	67
More fluid/dynamic structure of new strategic plan	63
Conducting more/different analyses	61
Planning for a shorter time frame	56
More regular, careful scrutiny of environmental metrics	47

The full article and survey are available on mckinseyquarterly.com.

Reader commentary on strategic planning

The virtues of scenario planning

"I'm somewhat disappointed by the moderate response to scenario planning. I would have thought more people would embrace it in these turbulent times, where any future is possible."
Victor Honadijy, *MD Anderson Cancer Center*, Houston, TX USA

"Scenario planning accounted for a large portion of our offsite planning this year. We focused on both long-term and short-term goals.

The major change we made in 2009, compared with previous years, is that we will be carefully reviewing and monitoring our progress against our strategic-action plans on a monthly basis and will have general reviews on a quarterly basis as well.

The frequent monitoring of progress against plans will be beneficial to our company in a sense that we can have more oversight on our corporate budget and spending, more control on CAPEX projects, more focus on growing revenue from the sales of products and services."
Rene Kakou, *Groupe Macrobell*, Montréal, QC Canada

Strategic planning—not the answer?

"This discussion is great, but misses a big issue—nearly all significant organizations already did 'strategic planning' in the run-up to the crisis, but virtually none saw it coming, prepared to avoid it, or had plans in place to cope with it."
Kim Warren

"Scenario planning assumes that some form of an envisaged future scenario may come to pass. This generally is no longer the case. We need to make use of Complex Adaptive Systems theory and new tools for strategy formulation. There are just too many Black Swans that may disrupt the future (the economic meltdown is a case in point). Scenario planning is not the answer."
Richard Weeks, *University of Pretoria*, South Africa

The value of business history

"Those who actually read and try to learn from business history—not only that of the US but also of other countries (especially the UK, Australia, Canada, and the Netherlands)—find that they are relatively well prepared for the current financial and political scene. History repeats, even if with a stutter; one does not need to be a genius nor very imaginative to see how similar scenes have played out historically and to imagine alternative scenarios arising from today's circumstances. Also, one often avoids making the same mistakes others did. The point is to get a truly longer-term perspective—about 100 years—not a five- or ten-year one. It may take some work, but for those who enjoy reading and are prepared to do the unpleasant task of thinking, the benefits are clear."
Joseph Tovey

"While a concept of learning from history has merit, I daresay that it often gets overwhelmed by the desire to 'ride the wave' when the going is good. Besides significantly enhancing the stature of economists, my fervent hope is that the current crisis will force the companies to temper their growth aspirations against sound governance principles."
Vinay Dixit

"Bad news is good news to the prepared. Every crisis/downturn presents opportunities to individuals and organizations that are prepared for them. Cash is king. Therefore, every company needs to balance its sources of cash—such as sales revenue and debt—with costs and expenses that consume cash.

I quite agree with the position of Joseph Tovey. It aligns with a classical definition of vision as 'foresight (seeing the future) based on insight (knowledge, ideas) with the benefit of hindsight (past experience, case studies, etc.).'"
Hilary Eledu, *BGL*, Nigeria

Personal experiences with strategic and scenario planning

"What I find startling is that even during this period of economic uncertainty, executives and administrators in the public sector (for example, in public health, academia, and associations) don't seem in touch with reality. There is no sense of urgency to redevelop plans and change the 'business.'

Some organizations—like people—have to be at the brink of collapse before they change. As the article alludes, the point is that the way we work must change, and it first begins in our mind-sets. Within an organization, a cultural mind shift is a critical yet important one to make that sometimes requires new leadership.

Unfortunately, when you keep old leadership—even with the best of intentions—they may not be prepared to handle the challenges nor be equipped with the skill set and mind-set to successfully complete the transition. That is the case with the lack of planning and strategy with many organizations, particularly in the public sector."
Tambra Stevenson

"A good strategy, a flexible business model that can absorb some shocks, good communication of the strategy to employees and stakeholders, and a good governance process with incentives aligned to the strategy are the basic recipe. Good tools can help, but it's the people, open minds, and open processes that matter most."
Eapen Chacko

Copyright © 2009 McKinsey & Company. All rights reserved.

We welcome your comments on this article. Please send them to quarterly_comments@mckinsey.com.

For more reader responses, visit mckinseyquarterly.com.

Frank Chimero

How 'animal spirits' destabilize economies

Textbook economics teaches that capitalism is essentially stable and has little need for government interference. That line of thinking is wrong.

George A. Akerlof and Robert J. Shiller

George Akerlof is the Koshland Professor of Economics at the University of California, Berkeley. He was awarded the 2001 Nobel Prize in economics.

Robert Shiller is the author of *Irrational Exuberance* and *The Subprime Solution*. He is also the Arthur M. Okun Professor of Economics at Yale University and is a fellow at the International Center for Finance, Yale School of Management.

For years, the world economy has been on a roller coaster. Yet not until it began to veer off the tracks did the passengers realize that they had embarked on a wild ride. Abetted by their thoughtlessness, the amusement park's management didn't set limits on how high they could go or even provide safety equipment.

Why didn't people recognize the warning signs until banks collapsed, jobs vanished, and millions of mortgages were foreclosed? The answer is simple. Textbook economics teaches the benefits—and only the benefits—of free markets. This belief system, which has flourished throughout the world, holds that capitalism is essentially stable and has little need for government interference. According to that line of reasoning, which dates back to Adam Smith, if people in free markets rationally pursue their own economic interests, they will exhaust all mutually beneficial opportunities to produce and exchange.

Even at the theory's worst, it deserves high marks, at least by the criterion of a schoolboy we overheard in a restaurant who was complaining about the C he had received on a spelling test, though 70 percent of his answers were correct. In fact, however, we believe that Adam Smith was basically right about the economic advantages of capitalism. But we also think that his theory fails to explain why the economy takes roller-coaster rides, and the takeaway message—that there is little need for government intervention—is simply wrong.

Adam Smith saw that human beings rationally pursue their economic interests, and his economic theories explain what happens when they do. But they are also guided by noneconomic motives—"animal spirits"—which Adam Smith and his followers largely ignore. Sometimes people are irrational, wrong, shortsighted, or evil; sometimes they act for action's sake; and sometimes they uphold noneconomic values like fairness, honor, or righteousness. As the economist John Maynard Keynes understood, "Our basis of knowledge for estimating the yield ten years hence of a railway, a copper mine, a textile factory, the goodwill of a patent medicine, an Atlantic liner, a building in the City of London amounts to little and sometimes to nothing." In such an uncertain world, many decisions "can only be taken as a result of animal spirits."[1]

Five aspects of these animal spirits affect the economy: confidence and the feedback mechanisms that amplify disturbances; the setting of wages and prices, which depend largely on attitudes about fairness; the temptation toward corrupt and antisocial behavior; the "money illusion," or confusion between the nominal and real level of prices (so that people, for example, often miss the fact that conservative investments may be risky in times of inflation); and the story of each person's life and the lives of others—stories that in the aggregate, as a national or international story, play an important economic role.

The current crisis stems from our changing level of confidence, from temptations, envy, resentment, illusions, and, especially, from changing stories about the economy—stories that first glorified financial "innovation" and then represented it as a con game. These intangibles explain why people paid small fortunes for houses in cornfields; why others financed those purchases; why the Dow Jones industrial average peaked above 14,000 and fell, little more than a year later, below 7,000; why the US unemployment rate rose by 4 percentage points in 24 months; why Bear Stearns was only (and barely) saved by a Federal Reserve bailout and Lehman Brothers collapsed; why many banks are underfunded; and why some totter on the brink, even after a bailout, and may yet vanish.

Animal spirits at play

Explanations that involve only small deviations from Adam Smith's system of pure economic rationality are clear because they are posed

[1] John Maynard Keynes, *The General Theory of Employment, Interest and Money*, New York: Macmillan, 1973 [1936], pp. 149–50, 161–2.

within a very well-understood framework. But this doesn't mean that small deviations describe how the economy really works. Economic theory should be derived not from them but from the large, observable deviations that actually occur. A description of how the economy really works must consider animal spirits.

Why are financial prices so volatile?
No one has ever made rational sense of the wild gyrations in financial prices—gyrations as old as financial markets themselves. The US stock market's real value rose over fivefold between 1920 and 1929 and then came all the way back down from 1929 to 1932. It doubled between 1954 and 1973 but fell by half from 1973 to 1974. It rose almost eightfold between 1982 and 2000 and then fell by half from 2000 to 2008. No one can explain these fluctuations rationally, even after the fact. Economists can sometimes justify the stock price changes of individual companies, but not aggregate stock price movements, which don't seem explicable by changes in interest rates, dividends, earnings, or anything else.

When the stock market tanks, the authorities try to restore public confidence by insisting that "the fundamentals of the economy remain strong." The authorities are right in the sense that, almost always, it is the stock market that has changed; the fundamentals haven't. How do we know that they couldn't generate these changes? If prices reflect fundamentals, they do so because those fundamentals are useful in forecasting future stock payoffs. In theory, stock prices predict the discounted value of future income streams: dividends or earnings. But stock prices are much more variable than the discounted streams of dividends or earnings they are supposed to predict.

> The current crisis stems from changing stories about the economy—stories that first glorified financial 'innovation' and then represented it as a con game

A person who claims that stock prices reflect information about future payoffs resembles a berserk weather forecaster in a town where temperatures are fairly stable. The forecaster predicts that on one day the temperature will be 150° F and on another day –100° F. Even if he has the mean right, he should be fired. Likewise, you should reject the notion that stock prices reflect predictions, based on economic fundamentals, about future earnings. Prices are much too variable.

Price changes do, however, seem to be correlated with social changes. The economists Andrei Shleifer and Sendhil Mullainathan have observed this phenomenon in Merrill Lynch advertisements. In the early 1990s, before the stock market bubble, Merrill ran advertisements showing a grandfather fishing with his grandson. The caption said: "Maybe you should plan to grow rich slowly." When the market peaked, around 2000, Merrill's dramatically changed ads showed a picture of a bull-shaped computer chip, with a caption that read: "Be Wired . . . Be Bullish." After the collapse, Merrill went back to the grandfather and grandson fishing. The caption advertised "Income for a lifetime."

Keynes compared the stock market to a competition that asks the contestants to pick the six prettiest faces from a hundred photographs. The prize goes to the person whose choices come closest to the whole group's average preferences. Of course, to win such a competition you shouldn't pick the faces you find prettiest. You should pick those you think others will find prettiest or, better yet, the faces you think that others will think that others will find prettiest. Investing in stocks often resembles that.

Red Delicious apples offer another metaphor. Hardly anyone really likes their taste, yet they have become, overwhelmingly, the best-selling apples in the United States. They tasted better in the 19th century, when a different apple was marketed under this name. As connoisseurs shifted to other varietals, growers, to salvage their profits, moved the Red Delicious apple into a new market niche. It became the inexpensive apple that people thought other people liked or that people thought other people thought other people liked. Most growers gave up on good flavor. Most Americans don't understand that an apple could be so debased.[2] Likewise with speculative investments: many people don't understand how much a company can change or how many ways it can be debased. Stocks that nobody believes in but keep their value are the Red Delicious apples of investment.

Bubbles and the confidence multiplier

Obviously, investors want to get rich quickly when the market soars and to protect themselves when it sags. If they buy or sell in reaction to stock price increases or decreases, that response can feed back into additional price changes in the same direction—a price-to-price

---

[2] Adrian Higgins, "Why the Red Delicious no longer is," *Washington Post*, August 5, 2005.

feedback. A vicious circle may prolong the cycle for a while. Eventually, the bubble bursts, since only expectations of further increases support it.

Price-to-price feedback may not suffice to create major asset price bubbles, but other forms of feedback—in particular, those between bubble-inflated asset prices and the real economy—reinforce it. This additional feedback increases the cycle's length and amplifies price-to-price effects. There are at least three sources of feedback from asset markets to the real economy. When stock and housing prices rise, people who own these assets have less reason to save. Feeling wealthier, they spend more. They may also count their stock market gains or housing appreciation in current savings.

Asset values also play an important role in determining investment levels. When the stock market falls, companies spend less on new factories and equipment. When the market for single-family homes falls, construction companies drop plans to build. Bankruptcies too can greatly influence investments in business and housing. When asset prices fall, debtors default, compromising the financial institutions that normally provide debt financing. When they become less willing to make loans, the price of the assets drops more. Such asset price movements feed into public confidence: the price-to-earnings-to-price feedback. By contrast, rising stock prices boost confidence. People buy more goods and services, so corporate profits go up and stock prices rise again. These mutually reinforcing positive feedbacks continue for a while, until the feedback—and the economy—head in the opposite direction.

Leverage feedback and the leverage cycle intensify other kinds of feedback. The collateral ratio is the amount lenders extend to investors as a percentage of the value of the assets posted as collateral. On the cycle's upswing, collateral ratios rise: for example, in the market for single-family homes, the amount banks lend to buyers (as a fraction of their homes' value) goes up. Rising leverage feeds back into asset price increases, encouraging still more leverage. As asset prices fall, the process works in reverse.

The leverage cycle operates in part because of bank capital requirements. As asset prices rise, the capital of leveraged financial institutions rises relative to their regulatory requirements, so they may buy more assets. If many do, they may bid prices up, freeing more capital. A feedback loop thus propels prices steadily higher. If asset prices fall, leveraged financial institutions may have to meet their capital requirements by selling. The systemic effect may be still-lower asset prices, which decrease capital ratios, so the institutions must sell yet more assets. In extreme cases, downward feedback pushes prices to fire sale levels.

For most people, the rise in real earnings that accompanies a stock market boom proves that the boom is rational. Few see that the earnings rise may be a temporary manifestation of the stock market rise. If rents go up during a housing-price boom, people think the increase justifies the boom. They don't consider the possibility that rising rents are a temporary manifestation of it.

Animal spirits and oil price movements

The price of oil too has fluctuated greatly—especially during the oil crisis years, 1973 to 1986. The first such crisis lasted from 1972 to 1974, when the Organization of Petroleum Exporting Countries (OPEC) restricted production. The price of crude oil more than doubled.

Ostensibly, OPEC was avenging the Arab defeat in the 1973 Yom Kippur War. But there is another, less well-known explanation. Before 1973, the anachronistically named Texas Railroad Commission regulated the fraction of time Texas oil producers could pump. These restrictions raised the price of oil. Little notice was taken in late 1972, when the quota rose to 100 percent. From then on, OPEC could restrict output to push up prices, and the United States couldn't increase output in response, since it was already as high as possible. In 1979, the Iran–Iraq War disrupted the supply of Persian Gulf oil, and prices doubled again, remaining high until 1986. Then, following the recession of the early 1980s, oil prices fell by half.

This summary seems to suggest that fundamentals—if not economic fundamentals, then political and military ones—determine oil prices. Indeed, these probably were the dominant factors then and ever since. Even so, feedbacks among confidence, production, and prices in the oil market strikingly resemble those in the stock market.

> Asking why capital expenditure fluctuates from year to year is a bit like asking why beer consumption fluctuates from one poker party to another

A crescendo of rhetoric about the population explosion and the shortages it would engender accompanied the rise of oil prices in the 1970s. Just 18 months before OPEC restricted production, *The Limits to Growth: A Report for the Club of Rome's Project on the Predicament of Mankind*[3] foretold worldwide economic disaster—in one scenario, the death of as much as half of the world's population late in the 21st century. Such thinking encouraged OPEC, whose ministers reasoned that reducing oil production would not only lead

---

[3] Donella H. Meadows, Dennis L. Meadows, Jorgen Randers, and William W. Behrens III, *The Limits to Growth: A Report for the Club of Rome's Project on the Predicament of Mankind*, New York: Universe Books, 1973.

to higher prices but also save the remaining oil for a day when prices would be higher still. Of course, OPEC's decision also confirmed the beliefs of those who concurred with the Club of Rome, a global think tank. What more dramatic proof could there be than a tripling of the price of oil? When the price fell in the wake of the recession of the early 1980s, the doomsday stories abated. A ProQuest search of the *New York Times*, the *Los Angeles Times*, and the *Washington Post* for articles containing the words "proven reserves" and "oil" yields 115 results from 1975 to 1979, 137 from 1980 to 1984—and only 73 from 1985 to 1989.

Resources are indeed limited. Global warming is a threat. But the price of oil and the stories about it resembled those about the stock market. Oil prices are variable. Again, the weather forecaster should be fired.

The markets as drivers of investment
A country's investment in new machinery and equipment, factories, bridges and highways, software, and communications infrastructure matters enormously for its economic prosperity. Careful studies have confirmed that such investments raise the standard of living.

Nonetheless, executives make them in the face of fundamental uncertainty. Theoretical economists who struggle to understand how people handle uncertainty seem to be converging on behavioral economics. *Jack: Straight from the Gut*, the title of the autobiography of former GE chairman Jack Welch, sums up this reality: investment decisions are intuitive, not analytical. Intuition, a social process, follows the laws of psychology—indeed, of social psychology. Asking why capital expenditure fluctuates from year to year is a bit like asking why beer consumption fluctuates from one poker party to another.

Given the speculative fluctuations in asset prices, variations in investment levels must partly reflect beliefs about these changing prices. As Welch writes, "The company's mood fluctuated on the bullishness of our press clippings and the price of our stock. Every positive story seemed to make the organization perk up. Every downbeat article gave the whimpering cynics hope."[4] To be sure, there is some doubt about the relation between stock prices and investment. According to a metric devised by the economists James Tobin and William Brainard, the correlation should be exact. In reality, it is weak.

The correlation holds for the crash years (1929 to the early 1930s) and for the millennium boom in the 1990s, when the market and investment rose and fell together. But there were two significant episodes

[4] Jack Welch with John A. Byrne, *Jack: Straight from the Gut*, New York: Warner, 2001, p. 172.

when the stock market declined while investment continued robustly. After World War II, the market tanked, yet the economy became so strong that inflation rose above 14 percent in 1947; investment was also high. A similar scenario unfolded after the first oil crisis. The data seem to imply that if the stock market falls because of inflation while the economy remains strong, investment probably will too.

Taming the beast: Making financial markets work for us

For decades, the dominant story about the economy maintained that all the fluctuations described previously had a rational basis. During the bubble years, the story also held that any risk arising from assets such as houses and subprime mortgages could be managed through complex financial devices like securitization and derivatives, which were largely unregulated. Then the story changed. The new one suggested that all this complexity was just a novel way of selling snake oil. As the new story about Wall Street and its products took hold, the life drained out of financial markets. Housing prices sank, the demand for exotic products collapsed, and the credit crunch began.

So once again, capitalism's dark side must be addressed. In the 1930s, in the wake of a huge catastrophe, the Roosevelt administration set up safeguards to protect the public from the excesses of free enterprise. For more than 70 years, those safeguards worked, but then complexity provided a way to evade regulation. Now there must be a new story about markets—a story that doesn't always predict sunshine. New financial regulations will be needed to acknowledge the animal spirits that often drive markets, to make markets work effectively, and to minimize the possibility that they will collapse and require vast bailouts at public expense.

Related articles on mckinseyquarterly.com
Taking improbable events seriously: An interview with the author of *The Black Swan*
Exploring business's social contract: An Interview with Daniel Yankelovich
Financial crisis and reform: Looking back for clues to the future

The present troubles aren't really a crisis of capitalism. Free enterprise is still the best way to supply most goods and services. But financial goods and services are different. Capitalism works well when people know and understand what they buy. Most people, however, know almost nothing about the financial products purchased on their behalf—for example, through pension funds, 401(k) accounts, money market funds, or, if they are very rich, hedge funds.

If we thought that human beings were totally rational and acted mainly from economic motives, we, like Adam Smith and his followers today, would believe that governments should play little role in regulating financial markets and perhaps even in determining aggregate demand. But on the contrary, we believe that animal spirits play a significant and largely destabilizing role. Without government intervention, employment levels will at times swing massively, financial markets will fall into chaos, scoundrels will flourish, and huge numbers of people will live in misery. The right answers may not always be clear. But our country has no chance of finding them if it doesn't acknowledge the importance of animal spirits. o

This article is adapted from George A. Akerlof and Robert J. Shiller's new book, *Animal Spirits: How Human Psychology Drives the Economy, and Why It Matters for Global Capitalism* (Princeton University Press, 2009).

Sandra Dionisi

Developing entrepreneurs among the world's poorest:
An interview with Acumen Fund's founder

Jacqueline Novogratz, CEO of venture-philanthropy firm Acumen Fund, discusses what the private sector can teach the public sector—and what it could stand to learn.

Bill Javetski

A finance leader turned social-sector pioneer, Jacqueline Novogratz used her business know-how to forge a new philanthropic approach. Through a mix of public work and private investment, Novogratz applied her brand of "venture philanthropy" to create Acumen Fund. Founded in 2001 with help from the Rockefeller Foundation and Cisco Systems Foundation, her organization has taken a decidedly market-based approach to developing entrepreneurs in the world's poorest countries. She recently sat down at Acumen's New York headquarters with Bill Javetski of the *Quarterly* to reflect on the successes and challenges of flipping traditional charity on its head, the growth opportunities she sees for Acumen, and the lessons in leadership she has learned from working in the social sector.

The *Quarterly*: *The philanthropic community is divided to some extent around the question of the private sector's role in helping the poor, particularly in the area of microfinance. Some would argue that there is no place in the philanthropic community for the private sector—that in some ways it's exploitive.*

Jacqueline Novogratz: I always get really nervous with absolutes in a world that is as messy as ours. When we started in 2001, the field was pretty uncrowded. We were pretty much the only player at the very beginning that was using philanthropic money to invest equity and loans in for-profit companies. Now, it's a crowded field. We're

Bill Javetski is a member of the *McKinsey Quarterly*'s board of editors.

seeing a spectrum of capital from grants to pure venture, and Acumen Fund is playing all along the way. But the question is, essentially, how do you take presumably the most flexible capital—philanthropic dollars—and invest it in a way so as to gain the most leverage, the most impact, and do so in the most efficient way possible?

What Acumen says is that we should use the market as a listening device and treat all people, no matter what their income level, as potential customers who want to make active decisions in their lives. If we can start with the more honest conversation that often comes from markets rather than from just gift giving, then we can learn the limitations of the market, and we can also learn where we reach our limits in extending service to the poor. That's when charity or government can really play a very important role. By using our philanthropy in a market-driven way, we can find where the efficiencies—as well as the public needs—lie.

The Quarterly: *How does that work in practice?*

Jacqueline Novogratz: One example would be the issue of safe drinking water. Currently, 1.2 billion people in the world don't have access to safe drinking water. I have been asked to speak at many

---

Jacqueline Novogratz

Vital statistics
Born March 15, 1961, in Fort Bragg, NC

Married

Education
Graduated with BA in economics and international relations in 1983 from the University of Virginia

Earned MBA in 1991 from Stanford University's Graduate School of Business

Career highlights
Acumen Fund (2001–present)
• Founder and CEO

Rockefeller Foundation
• Director of special projects (1994–2001)
• Fellow (1991–92)

Chase Manhattan Bank (now Chase) (1983–86)
• International credit analyst; assistant treasurer

Fast facts
Founded and directed the Philanthropy Workshop (1995) and the Next Generation Leadership (1997) programs at the Rockefeller Foundation, and founded Duterimbere (1987), a microfinance institution in Rwanda

Serves on advisory boards of Stanford Graduate School of Business and of *Innovations* journal (MIT Press); on board of trustees for Aspen Institute; and is a member of two of the World Economic Forum's Global Agenda Councils (social entrepreneurship and water security)

Is an Aspen Institute Henry Crown Fellow and a Synergos Institute Senior Fellow

Received Ernst & Young Metro New York Entrepreneur of the Year award (2008), Leadership in Social Entrepreneurship award from CASE at Duke University (2009)

Visit mckinseyquarterly.com to watch a series of video interviews with Jacqueline Novogratz.

conferences where the dialectic is, "Is safe water a human right and therefore should it be distributed free to all people, or should it be privatized?" Frankly, I am incredibly frustrated by these conceptual theoretical conversations.

So we identified an incredible entrepreneur, Tralance Addy. He was a Ghanaian living in Los Angeles and wanted to build a company in India to test whether it was feasible to sell safe water to low-income rural people in Andhra Pradesh. In the state, there were many politicians that told us, "Our policy is free water for all." My response was, "You have 200 million people in the country who have no access to water and upwards of 400 million people who have extremely limited access, so maybe a little experiment wouldn't be such a bad thing."

We used our patient capital—money that most investors would not have at risk but that, at the same time, would not necessarily generate high returns—to put $600,000 into a start-up company that was using ultraviolet filtration technology to filter village swamp water and make it available to low-income people. There was a lot of experimentation. We went to the commercial banks, which wouldn't lend to the entrepreneurs without a guarantee. We used our patient capital to put up a 30 percent first-loss guarantee. And, over a couple of years, we proved to the banks that our estimates of loss were actually much too conservative. When we negotiated a second guarantee of facilities, we only had to take a 15 percent first-loss guarantee. And we're hoping that will continue to move down.

Today, WaterHealth International reaches about 350,000 paying customers in 200 villages and projects that it will be serving more than a million customers in the next two to three years. So suddenly we have an example of what it takes to deliver affordable, quality water to low-income people in rural areas, which is bashing a lot of stereotypes and providing a model—not the only model, but one model—for ways in which the world might think more creatively and constructively about bringing affordable services to the poor so they can make their own choices.

The Quarterly: *What have you learned about the challenges and the opportunities involved in scaling up some of these businesses?*

Jacqueline Novogratz: There are three critical factors: leadership, which is the most important; sustainability, which addresses whether you can cover your costs in time; and then, finally, scalability. For shorthand, just in terms of operational efficiency, we focus on whether we fully believe that an enterprise can reach at least a million customers, so we then have a model we can take to the world.

Some of the opportunities to scale would be in East Africa—recognizing that if 92 percent of the malaria cases are in Africa, then why not find those opportunities to invest in entrepreneurs in Africa to provide services and products for Africans? Some of the challenges to scale often involve the entrepreneur herself or himself. They're comfortable getting the organization to a certain level, but then sometimes—because of philosophical reasons, because they're scared, or because they don't feel capable—they can't get to that next level.

Capital is obviously another major constraint to scale. I would say at the beginning we erred on generosity. We were patient capital. We were the nice guys that were going to help you build. And we learned that this approach worked at the beginning, but then, when we wanted to get to the table and bring in other, more traditional investors that were needed to scale the enterprise, our generosity actually worked against the organization. Now we have to think through—in much more market-oriented terms than when we started—what kind of capital structure would give an enterprise the best possible chance of success.

So those are two of the major constraints. The third—which happens, unfortunately, more than I would like—is when the success of a particular enterprise is threatening to local politicians, in which case policy can really come in and make it very difficult for the organization to succeed.

The Quarterly: *What about the economic crisis? What has been its impact on your organization and the philanthropic community at large?*

Jacqueline Novogratz: In the philanthropic sector, I think we are seeing a lot of fear, a lot of pulling back, a lot of, "I don't have enough to give." But we're also seeing a lot of people who recognize that when the rich stumble, the poor can't fall off a cliff. And they are still giving—though not necessarily at the same levels that they were, because they feel less secure. It's interesting on a market-by-market basis that in some ways, when you look at a country like Pakistan, there was really no mortgage market to speak of. So you don't see the same levels of crisis from within.

On the other hand, you are seeing the lowest levels of society—particularly if they're in any export-driven business, and I'm including exporting from the slums into the city center—facing higher prices. In countries like Pakistan, inflation rates are as high as 27 percent. If you hire anybody, it's very difficult to meet those margins.

So it's a very tense time for low-income people. On other hand, our companies sell the basics: food, health, water. And people are still finding ways to get them, which is why our investments—while they may be slightly slowing—are still quite robust. So it's a mixed bag. It's not completely straightforward.

The Quarterly: *How do you see Acumen growing in the coming years?*

Jacqueline Novogratz: I think the question for Acumen now is, "What will we be best at?" There's the investing work we do, there's the talent work we do, there's the knowledge and communications work we do. Growth is an absolute for us, in part because of this desire to constantly reevaluate the way we look at delivering services to the poor. The question is, "How much growth?" And then the next question is, "How do we also emphasize the rest of what Acumen Fund does?"

So for Acumen, if our first eight years were focused in large part on investing—on understanding how to invest in these markets that have high levels of corruption, very poor levels of distribution, and almost no marketing—then maybe the next ten years are equally about developing talent, developing the stories that inspire and influence a generation to believe that we can do things differently in the world. We don't have to be sitting just within the marketplace nor just within traditional philanthropy or charity. There is real room for reinventing an economy that is global but that is also more imaginative, creative, and, most important, inclusive.

> 'What I love about finance—and even what I love about accounting—is that it's another form of storytelling'

What I hope these next years will bring is an opportunity for Acumen Fund to influence more young people about what leadership can look like in this century. We are barraged with resumes from young people, as well as from people in their 50s, 60s, and 70s, who want to do something different with their lives. But they don't want to work in a traditional charity. They want to use their skills in finance, marketing, and accounting to contribute to the world.

The Quarterly: *You've succeeded as a leader in both the financial sector and the social sector. Any thoughts on the differences, and why we see fewer women leaders in finance?*

Jacqueline Novogratz: What I love about finance—and even what I love about accounting, which is kind of embarrassing to admit—is that it's another form of storytelling. If you could teach young people to find stories in the combination of the balance sheet and the income statement, I think we would see a lot more girls taking on leadership roles and finding that comfort.

I recently did a panel for women who work on Wall Street, and what they spoke about was how rigid our financial institutions continue to be around integrating women into the workforce—particularly after they've had children—and that the rules are so driven by a traditional kind of discipline. This is a discipline that the social sector has taken upon itself to reinvent. And that may be more to the point as to why we don't see as many women leaders in finance. It's a much older club. It's been driven by a stricter set of rules and expectations.

Related articles on mckinseyquarterly.com
Developing entrepreneurship among the world's poorest
The state of corporate philanthropy: A McKinsey Global Survey
Women and leadership: Learning from the social sector

I have four brothers who all work on Wall Street, and I remember when my brother's wife had a child. I said, "Well, is there paternity leave?" And he said, "Oh, yeah. We have the most liberal paternity leave on Wall Street—but I would never take it, because if I did, everybody would think I was, you know, wimpy." And I think there's great truth to that. So there's a cultural piece that needs to be looked at. Whereas in the social sector, as a woman leader, you have the opportunity to invent the culture in which you want to work and thrive.

The Quarterly: *What specific lessons in leadership have you learned from the social sector, particularly through your work in developing other entrepreneurs?*

Jacqueline Novogratz: In 1986, I went to Rwanda, where I worked with a small group of women to start the first microfinance organization in the country and, simultaneously, a bakery with 20 unwed mothers. I went in as a leader with pure audaciousness. I just assumed, "I can do the Bad News Bears thing really well; I'm just going to cheer them on"—without having the humility of really understanding what their starting place was. I had to learn to have the humility myself to really listen to their perspectives, and yet not stop there; to have the audaciousness to say, "It's a good starting point, but we want to get you to this other place."

Copyright © 2009 McKinsey & Company. All rights reserved.

We welcome your comments on this article. Please send them to quarterly_comments@mckinsey.com.

The real lesson for me was that dignity is so much more important to the human spirit than wealth. And that what these women needed—as all of us do—was to know that they could cover their basic needs and yet still have the power to say no to work that they didn't want to do. And so I think of true leadership as a way of inspiring, listening, and letting people grow themselves in their own way.

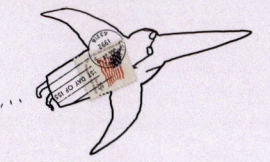

Letters to the Editor

Reader comments on Jacqueline Novogratz's interview from mckinseyquarterly.com.

The interview with Jacqueline Novogratz, CEO of the Acumen Fund, is a very revealing example of the continuing paternal (or perhaps maternal) attitudes that aid agencies have been criticized about for decades. It is sad to see it promoted by an otherwise excellent agency.

The suggestion that a "private sector" approach to charging interest for services is the way forward, and that charities are not good at trading is just patently wrong. Microfinance has been embraced and extended by charities, to many areas never previously envisaged and in ways that could not be contemplated within the constraints of a straightforward repayment system.

Privately funded initiatives—whilst very welcome in offering alternatives and additional funding—need to work in partnership with agencies that know and understand the problems they are trying to solve and can do it without patronizing and disempowering the beneficiaries.

Peter Maple
Chief Executive, *Kew Quorum*
United Kingdom

What has struck me are Jacqueline Novogratz's dogged persistence, and her incremental additions of different aspects of a good business model. She didn't give up, and she resolved issues as they arose. Her hands-on approach also demonstrates her commitment and involvement.

There are many lessons here for struggling nonprofits.

Rina Kamath
Founder and CEO, *Cause Humane Integrated Professional Services*
Mumbai, India

Alleviating poverty overseas is extremely difficult, and nobody involved in it over the past 40 or so years should be arrogant enough to think they have right answers. So, I was impressed by the Acumen approach, which clearly emphasises learning and a willingness to adjust procedures to fit the circumstances. I see nothing arrogant or paternalistic in this. Indeed, fresh thinking should be welcomed. I don't think that Acumen has much to learn from those who have been around in the field a long time.

Brian Scott
Former CEO, *Oxfam Ireland*
Belfast, Northern Ireland

Jacqueline's efforts try to address the problem of charities that do not work on profit motives, and are good. However, in third-world countries the problems which have arisen in the first place are due to illiteracy, the absence of government schools which provide quality education to the poor, and the lack of programs which help children develop skills so that they can stand on their own feet.

The focus of the charities can be to take over government schools and provide quality education for children studying there, among other things.

Only education can provide a lasting solution for the highlighted problem.

Sathyavageeswaran P
Consultant, *Morison Menon*
Bangalore, India

Visit mckinseyquarterly.com for more reader responses to this article.

Enduring Ideas
Classic McKinsey frameworks that continue to inform management thinking

The portfolio of initiatives

Level of familiarity/risk

Familiar
Company's distinctive knowledge surpasses that of competitors

Unfamiliar
Company's knowledge is surpassed by that of competitors

Uncertain
Probability of success difficult to determine

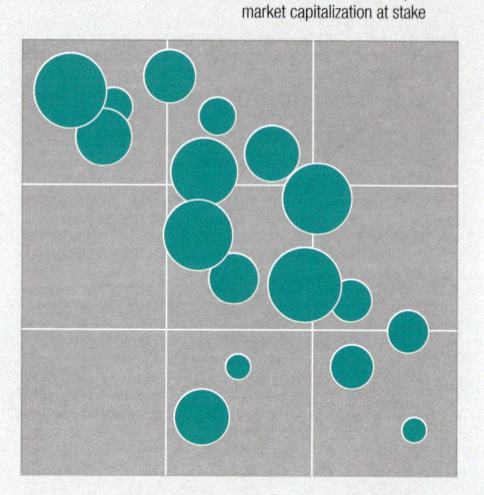

● Size of initiative indicates potential market capitalization at stake

Time

Short term Initiatives contribute to current earnings

Medium term Initiatives mature in 2 to 3 years

Long term Initiatives mature in 3+ years

Classic approaches to business strategy assume a foreseeable future based on reasonable assumptions about developments in markets, technologies, or regulation. In an increasingly uncertain world, this approach falls short. The portfolio-of-initiatives framework, developed in the early 2000s by McKinsey director Lowell Bryan, drawing on ideas such as the three horizons of growth and Hugh Courtney's levels of uncertainty, offers a way to develop strategy in a more fluid, less predictable environment. In the 2002 *McKinsey Quarterly* article "Just-in-time strategy for a turbulent world," Bryan compares such a portfolio to a convoy of ships in wartime: their numbers and diversity improve the likelihood of survival for any one of them.

The framework takes into consideration two aspects of initiatives: familiarity and time. Initiatives that allow a company to deploy a large amount of distinctive knowledge give it the advantage of familiarity and the possibility of reaping superior rewards for a given level of risk. Such initiatives warrant the largest commitment of resources. Next come initiatives that require a company to acquire certain kinds of knowledge. In developing initiatives over time, a company must have enough of them not only to ensure large current returns but also to place bets that could help it grow in the medium and long terms.

To apply the portfolio-of-initiatives approach, companies must take three steps: undertake a disciplined search for a number of initiatives that provide high rewards for the risks taken; monitor the resulting portfolio rigorously, reinvesting in successes and terminating failures; and take a flexible, evolutionary approach allowing for midcourse corrections. The resulting strategy, like a conscious form of natural selection, identifies the strongest initiatives and sheds the rest. The increasing uncertainty of today's business environment and the importance of balancing risks with rewards make the portfolio-of-initiatives framework more relevant than ever.

Copyright © 2009 McKinsey & Company. All rights reserved.

Artwork by Leigh Wells